# Endorsements

Mario Murillo is a firebrand for revival. In this critical hour for our nation, Mario's new book releases a sobering wake-up call for the Church in America. I believe Christians everywhere need to take this message to heart, because it will ignite boldness to stand for God's truth and engage culture in the power of the Holy Spirit. This book is a must-read.

Dr. Ché Ahn
President, Harvest International Ministry
Senior Pastor, Harvest Rock Church, Pasadena, CA
International Chancellor, Wagner University

There are those that the Lord raises up as voices crying out preparing the way of the Lord. They are anointed in the earth to know the times as well as what the nations are to do. Mario is one that is carrying both the clear sound of the Lord and His heart in this day. Now is NOT the time to be silent as future generations need our courageous voices standing for what is right and true. Mario's new book, *Do Not Leave Quietly*, is full of heart-checking, fire-filled pages with the spirit of revival and reformation. I challenge you to not only read and apply what is written but to share a copy with others. When you do, you will align yourself to a moral awakening that is in our midst and a reversal of the damage of passive Christianity, a woke culture and the carefully plotted

Marxist's agenda to steal our freedoms and silence the Church of the Lord Jesus Christ.

HANK KUNNEMAN, Senior Pastor
Lord of Hosts Church and One Voice Ministries
Omaha, NE

Today we are living in a time when woke is applauded and socialism/border-line communism is embraced by a large part of America. The sad truth is it is even found in the Church.

Now is the time for all Americans and especially those in the Church to wake up and respond to this agenda with a resounding "NO!"

There's only one Mario Murillo and in this book Mario does an excellent job breaking down what is going on in our world and what we should do when in response as only Mario can. The days of leaving quietly are indeed over. This book is a rallying cry for believers to stand up and make our voices heard. Revival is at hand and an Awakening is already in process across America.

This book will challenge you, encourage you and prod you into your calling for "such a time as this." When we started FlashPoint we knew God was igniting passion in people around the world. This book does exactly that. Turn the page and enjoy the ride.

GENE BAILEY
Host, *Flashpoint*
Author of *Flashpoint of Revival*

# Do Not
# LEAVE
# QUIETLY

OTHER DESTINY IMAGE BOOKS BY
MARIO MURILLO

*Vessels of Fire and Glory*

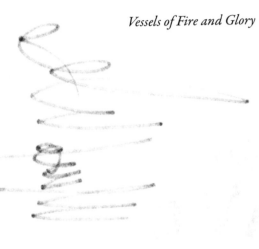

# Do Not
# LEAVE
# QUIETLY

*A Call for*
*Everyday People to*
*Rise Up & Defeat Evil*

# MARIO MURILLO

DESTINY IMAGE® PUBLISHERS, INC.

P.O. Box 310, Shippensburg, PA 17257-0310

*"Promoting Inspired Lives."*

This book and all other Destiny Image and Destiny Image Fiction books are available at Christian bookstores and distributors worldwide.

For more information on foreign distributors, call 717-532-3040.

Reach us on the Internet: www.destinyimage.com.

ISBN 13 TP: 978-0-7684-5919-7
ISBN 13 eBook: 978-0-7684-5920-3
ISBN 13 HC: 978-0-7684-5922-7
ISBN 13 LP: 978-0-7684-5921-0

For Worldwide Distribution, Printed in the U.S.A.

1 2 3 4 5 6 7 8 / 26 25 24 23 22

# CONTENTS

# FOREWORD

A MOVEMENT HAS BEGUN. HISTORICALLY, AMERICAN AWAK-enings precede a crisis, like the Edwards and Whitfield revivals leading up to the American Revolution or the Finney revivals before the Civil War. Sometimes they follow, such as the revivals in 1948 after WWII.

What is happening now is an Awakening of a different sort; it occurs *during* a crisis of national unraveling. An unraveling made up of issues that are not just cultural but political because politics has become the ultimate enforcer of morality in an all-or-nothing, zero-sum game of power. Those who said, "you can't legislate morality," were wrong. You can't make someone righteous by legislation, but you can legalize lawlessness and persecute the righteous by lawless decrees. This awakening is on a collision course with these lawless powers engineering America's collapse. It is inevitable that the Kingdom of God will collide with forces destroying the nation. The new awakeners are not engaging in politics because they are political; instead, they push back on government because the political sphere became religious. The new awakeners didn't choose to get involved with politics; politics decided to get involved with them when it transgressed into the territory of religious liberty.

In such an hour when the situation is desperate, but the saints are not, God sent a man named Mario Murillo. No armchair evangelist could have written this book. Its pages breathe with the fire of someone on the front lines of the conflict. Mario wrote while tending the fires of this very awakening. He has had to expand his tent as thousands find their way, often across fields and through rain and biting cold to get to his meetings. In Mario's tent and writing, he pulls no punches. The gospel is preached, and signs and wonders break forth to confirm the supernatural power behind the message. Multitudes come to the altar, sometimes more than once in the same meeting. His message in the tent and in this book is nothing less than a battle cry for saving America! Perhaps one of the elements that compelled me most was that in upstate New York, during one of Mario's crusades, over a thousand pastors and leaders gathered together, moving as one, to take on the battle for seeing transformation in their state. If meetings like these are indicators of what's rumbling in the Church, truly a remnant is rising up, unified, organized, and committed to push back against the insidious agendas seeking to disciple our nation.

At the passing of Billy Graham, I witnessed an unusual convergence. I recalled how a prophet and friend of mine named Kim Clement spoke of God raising new vessels with the anointing of Billy Graham. I thought of this as another instrument of providence named Donald Trump tapped on the pinewood coffin of the great statesman evangelist, lying in the capitol of Washington D.C. The President prayed that God would raise a new generation of male and female Billy Grahams. I believe Mario carries an anointing that answers both Kim's prophecy and the President's prayer. Furthermore, I think others will light their torch from the torch he carries.

In these days of Americas Revolution, Mario's manuscript will have the same effect as Thomas Paine's pamphlets to the Continental army. Paine's booklet *Common Sense* breathed such life into Washington that he insisted his officers read it to his soldiers during the brutal winter of Valley Forge 1776. Those words inspired Washington. As a result, he decided to turn the long tide of colonial defeat into a stunning, unexpected victory by crossing the frozen Delaware river and smashing the Hessian army in a surprise Christmas Eve attack. The psychological effect of this victory shifted all 13 colonies and reinvigorated the entire war effort, leading to ultimate success.

Mario is a prophet with a pen, an evangelist with a message and a prototype, the forerunner of a move of God on the eve of a great comeback in our second American Revolution.

Dr. Lance Wallnau
Bestselling Author of *God's Chaos Code*

# READ THIS FIRST

ONE DAY WITHIN THE NEXT FIVE YEARS, SOMETHING SHOCK-ing will happen to America. It will not be a war or a terrorist attack. It will not be a natural or an economic disaster. Instead, it will be a revealing.

On that day, wokeness, socialism, and progressivism will suddenly be revealed. Their true intentions will be known as they rip off their mask and openly declare war on the Church and the Bible.

Marxists could not come clean about this all at once. America had to be made ready to burn Bibles and arrest Christians. But we are almost there.

Maybe you have heard that 29 percent of Democrats now believe the unvaccinated should be placed in concentration camps. It will be a very small step to program them to hate believers in the same way they hate their fellow citizens.

I think of woke pastors. How humiliated they will be on that day. They only quote the Bible occasionally. What will they do when they can't quote it at all? Not even the easy-to-take-out-of-context verses they cherish.

Imagine their shame as they watch the Word of God, which they once denigrated, being incinerated. Think of their horror when they realize that they helped to push the American Church underground. Even the Marxists have a higher regard for the Bible than woke pastors do.

In fact, the Left must consider the Bible the most powerful book in the world. Look at all they felt they had to wreck before targeting the Holy Scriptures. They had to damage marriage, family, gender, citizenship, the economy, race relations, education, freedom of speech, and medical rights. Only then were they ready to take on the Bible.

But I see something else on the horizon. I see a vast moral awakening. It is powerful enough to reverse the damage of 40 years of Marxist planning. It has the potential to restore morality, common sense, and the fear of God.

We are at an inescapable fork in the road. We must choose the Christianity that forged American freedom or be cast into the black hole of Marxism.

If we leave quietly, there is no hope.

What matters to you? Your family, your freedoms, your plans for the future? Well, they all hinge on winning this war. Leaving quietly is the greatest threat to everything you love.

You must fully grasp what it means to leave quietly. You must see it in all its subtle and lethal forms. You need to blasted free of the gravitational pull of our depraved culture and the lukewarm Church. This is not a bad habit you work on. It is a beast that you must kill!

Finally, do not ask this book to ignite the fire. Bring the fire to the book. Open Chapter 1 with your spirit ablaze. Start reading with a heart that is already irrevocably committed to removing satan's filthy claws off of the throat of America.

Mario Murillo

# WHAT IS AT STAKE

*I never work better than when I am inspired by anger; when I am angry, I can write, pray, and preach well, for then my whole temperament is quickened, and my understanding sharpened, and all mundane vexations and temptations depart.*
—MARTIN LUTHER

Chapter 1

# YES, I AM ANGRY—YOU BETTER BE ANGRY TOO

YES, I AM ANGRY. I AM ANGRY AND DISGUSTED BY PREACHERS who are silent. They have no excuse.

Their silence during this sweeping destruction of morals and freedom makes them traitors.

I rage against the Leftist politicians for giving themselves over to evil, utterly. Turning America into a cesspool of hate, racism, perversion, crime, and murder. As a preacher, people ask me all the time when will I stop attacking the Democrat Party? The answer is simple. When they stop lying about Christianity, I will stop telling the truth about them.

I am nauseated by millions of apathetic, biblically illiterate Christians who have embraced values that God hates.

And I am even more ashamed of many Spirit-filled believers. Because I hold them to a higher standard. Too many of them play tricks with the prophetic and with the sacred gifts of the Spirit.

9

They dabble in the power of God, never asking themselves why God gave them power in the first place. Thus, they are violating both their duty and their mission.

Even many revivalists are not innocent. Leaders whip up a frenzy. Singing the same phrase over and over again. They sing about what they'll do to the devil someday. Belting out lyrics about all the authority they have over evil. But somehow, they never getting around to using it to save America.

Am I right to be angry? Yes, I am. And you better be too.

The right kind of anger is a very good thing. Mental health experts Todd Kashdan and Robert Biswas-Diener agree: "Anger is best viewed as a tool that helps us read and respond to upsetting social situations. Research overwhelmingly indicates that feeling angry increases optimism, creativity, effective performance—and research suggests that expressing anger can lead to more successful negotiations, in life or on the job."[1]

Even Paul the apostle said, "Be angry, and do not sin: do not let the sun go down on your wrath, nor give place to the devil" (Eph. 4:26-27). The right kind of anger is crucial in this hour.

Kashan and Diener went on to say, "Altruism is often born from anger; when it comes to mobilizing other people and creating support for a cause, no emotion is stronger. It's a mistake to presume that kindness, compassion, love, and fairness line up on one side of a continuum, and anger, rage, and dislike, on another side. Positivity alone is insufficient to the task of helping us navigate social interactions and relationships. A healthy society is not an anger-free society."[2]

And I am telling you that an anger-free Church is not a healthy Church. I would go even further. If you can look at what they are doing to American children and not feel anger, then you are a deeply flawed human being. Bearded men in dresses reading stories to them? Loony parents making videos of four-year-olds who want to change their gender?

Maybe that is still not enough to make you angry. Perhaps you still think I am being too hard on preachers and the Church. Maybe this will help:

A 14-year-old boy tells his school that he is a girl. He wins permission to use the girl's bathroom, then proceeds to enter the girl's bathroom, and there he rapes a young girl.

The girl's father went to the school to report the rape. They insisted they would take care of the investigation and told him not to tell the police.

When they did nothing about the rape, he went to the school board meeting and tried to confront them. They cut him off from speaking and lied, saying there was no report of a rape. The father exploded in rage and the board had the father arrested. There's more.

After the father was arrested, Leftists flooded social media with hate messages against the entire family and called him a right-wing bigot. The family actually went into hiding. And there's still more.

Because the rapist was a "trans" student, woke school officials quietly sent him to another school. They did not inform the new school the boy was a rapist. Once there, he raped another young girl. This is the spirit that currently controls our educational system. Are you angry yet?

I want to refer back to something that Todd Kashdan and Robert Biswas-Diener said about anger: "When it comes to mobilizing other people and creating support for a cause, no emotion is stronger."

We have a very clear example of this in the Bible. In 1 Samuel 11, a gangster terrorist—Nahash the Ammonite—overwhelmed the vulnerable Jewish outpost of Jabesh Gilead, and the villagers had no choice but to surrender.

Nahash was so vile that even after the people offered themselves to him as slaves, it was not enough. Remember the father whose daughter was raped? That wasn't enough for the Left. They piled it on until the victims were the villains. How dare anyone oppose the woke agenda?

Nahash said he would let them live, but only if he could put out their right eyes. He said he wanted to shame Israel. He was spoiling for a fight. You need to see that the Left is also bloodthirsty for a shot at Christianity.

The village fathers made one last desperate request in verse 3:

> Then the elders of Jabesh said to him, "Hold off for seven days, that we may send messengers to all the territory of Israel. And then, if there is no one to save us, we will come out to you."

Here is what happened next.

> So the messengers came to Gibeah of Saul and told the news in the hearing of the people. And all the people lifted up their voices and wept. Now there was Saul, coming behind the herd from the field; and Saul said, "What troubles the people, that they weep?" And they told him the words of the men of Jabesh. Then the Spirit

> *of God came upon Saul when he heard this news, and his anger was greatly aroused. So he took a yoke of oxen and cut them in pieces, and sent them throughout all the territory of Israel by the hands of messengers, saying, "Whoever does not go out with Saul and Samuel to battle, so it shall be done to his oxen"* (1 Samuel 11:4-7).

Saul cutting up his prize oxen back then is the equivalent of a televangelist taking a chainsaw to his Bentley today.

Here is what you must take from these verses. The anger came from the Holy Spirit, and Saul's act of sacrifice galvanized a nation. Verse 7 says, "And the fear of the Lord fell on the people, and they came out with one consent." Suddenly, there were 330,000 soldiers who were ready to fight for Israel. Nahash and his hordes were annihilated and Jabesh Gilead was saved.

The American Church needs to mobilize. Righteous indignation is the key. It starts right here, right now. A volcanic passion must burn within you. A fire within that burns away the trivial distractions and hesitations. A flame that vaporizes excuses and fear and gives way to a blazing clarity of purpose.

Martin Luther said, "I never work better than when I am inspired by anger; when I am angry, I can write, pray, and preach well, for then my whole temperament is quickened, and my understanding sharpened, and all mundane vexations and temptations depart."

## NOTE

1. Todd Kashdan and Robert Biswas-Diener, "The Right Way to Get Angry," *Greater Good Magazine*, October 20, 2014,

https://greatergood.berkeley.edu/article/item/the_right_way
_to_get_angry.

2. Ibid.

# Chapter 2

# SPEAK NOW, OR FOREVER HOLD YOUR PEACE

THIS IS THE CLEAREST WARNING GOD HAS EVER GIVEN ME. God is emphatically telling the American Church, "Speak now, or forever hold your peace." Whatever we are going to say, whatever we are going to do, whatever action we are going to take to protect our rights as Christians and Americans, we must do now.

Doubt my words at your own peril. Churches are about to be closed forever. People of faith will soon be marginalized, both socially and economically. What we are talking about here is the destruction of your children's and your grandchildren's future. They will live in a world where they will be targeted for the faith you have given them. And the worst part is that you will not be here to protect them when they endure the worst of it.

Listen closely—the threat I am describing is not years away, it is not even months away, it is days away. Yes, absolutely, we are days away from the new excuse the Democrats are preparing to use to wipe out the First, Second, Third, and Fourth Amendments to the Constitution.

Here is what has happened to justify the urgency of my writing. Satan has been working on this masterstroke of tyranny for years. The tapestry of lies he has woven is the greatest manipulation of truth in all of history.

> *Woe to those who call evil good, and good evil; who put darkness for light, and light for darkness* (Isaiah 5:20).

Their lies change hatred into love and love into hatred. They make racism equality and equality racism. The Left has changed the definition of so many terms that there are few, if any, words that carry their original meanings.

The web of evil that has fallen over all of America is clearly described in Isaiah 59:4-8:

> *No one calls for justice, Nor does any plead for truth. They trust in empty words and speak lies; They conceive evil and bring forth iniquity. They hatch vipers' eggs and weave the spider's web; He who eats of their eggs dies, And from that which is crushed a viper breaks out.*
>
> *Their webs will not become garments, Nor will they cover themselves with their works; Their works are works of iniquity, And the act of violence is in their*

*hands. Their feet run to evil, And they make haste to shed innocent blood; Their thoughts are thoughts of iniquity; Wasting and destruction are in their paths. The way of peace they have not known, And there is no justice in their ways; They have made themselves crooked paths; Whoever takes that way shall not know peace.*

That passage describes exactly what is happening, from our lowest back alleys to our highest offices of power.

And the following verses tell us what is coming next.

*Justice is turned back, And righteousness stands afar off; For truth is fallen in the street, And equity cannot enter. So truth fails, And he who departs from evil makes himself a prey* (Isaiah 59:14-15).

The moment you will become the prey of Marxist wolves is even now at the door.

*I am sick to death with those who refuse to call the Church to action.* Let me put it plainly. You have two choices: either cast your votes to restore Democracy to America, or make a plan to move your family to somewhere safe. I am also sick of those pastors who refuse to come to this obvious conclusion.

When you hear them screaming, "Mario Murillo is an extremist!" remember that we got to this point of desperation because of the lukewarm voices who refused to admit the approach of danger.

- Remember when California told us not to use our Bibles? Pastors did not galvanize a resistance to stop it.

- Remember when marriage was destroyed? Again, there was no national firewall of righteous leaders to intervene.

- Then they told us to close our churches, even as they condoned mass protests that led to violence and helped spread the virus. Again, there was no unanimous action from American church leaders.

- Then they told us that we cannot sing. Telling us that we must stop worshiping God was a test balloon to see how fast they can force the Church underground.

So what is next? Will they pass laws to extend the church-gathering ban indefinitely? Will they move on to dictating not only when we can meet, when we can sing, but will they also dictate what we can say? Will we finally find ourselves being ordered to read from a script that will be, in effect, a repudiation of our faith in Christ?

Remember, we are here because of an incurably wrong-headed sense of political correctness. Well, my brothers and sisters, that season is over. The gloves must come off. The righteous must rise up with a single roar—a noise that is unified and unending must rise from the Church!

*For years we have been told to just sit back and let it happen.* We were told that it was "all in God's hands," even as we ignored God's words. God has chosen to honor prayer. *God rewards those who seek to stand in the gap against national evil.*

Borrowing one last verse from Isaiah, which tells us our great predicament: *"Then the Lord saw it, and it displeased Him that there was no justice. He saw that there was no man, and wondered that there was no intercessor"* (Isa. 59:15-16).

God is shocked, and rightly so, that the American Church is still wandering, wavering, and weakening in the face of an invading enemy.

And yet, there is great hope because God's army is rising and its numbers are growing at this very hour. Notable Christian leaders are no longer worried about protecting their reputations, but are taking up a new anointing—a nation-saving anointing!

With every atom of my being, I am exhorting you to take action. To those who have no stomach for war and are oblivious of the fact that we are already at war, please spare me your empty excuses.

The American Church must rise up *now*. We are about to be bound and gagged by a rogue government.

Whatever confidence you have in my ministry—whatever level of trust I have earned—must now be put on the line.

Join us in this great struggle! Join a cause so noble and right that it is beyond belief that every Christian in America is not involved. This is the hour. You will never pass this way again.

Speak now, Church, or forever hold your peace!

# Chapter 3

# SILENCE LIKE A CANCER GROWS

WHAT ARE YOU FACING? YOU ARE FACING A NATION THAT has fallen in love with Communism. In fact, much of the infrastructure associated with Communism is already operating in our government.

What does America's lurch toward Communism mean to you? It means you will no longer own private property, and it means the end of the Bill of Rights. And that is only the beginning.

How can Americans feel an attraction to such a bankrupt ideology? Communism is the perfect poison. It is the polar opposite of everything we hold dear and everything that made us great, free, and prosperous.

The attraction to Communism is even more baffling when you consider that wherever it has been tried, it has been a spectacular failure. Never has a cure been this much worse than the disease. How can anyone still believe in something that has never worked and has only brought misery?

The answer is—hate. Karl Marx wrote *The Communist Manifesto* out of hate. Hate oozes from Communism's every pore and stokes its fires of revolution. And only hatred can keep it going.

For Communism to exist it must kill freedom, hope, and faith. But it also kills people by the millions. When Communism arrives, there is massive bloodshed. You cannot install Communism without committing heinous acts. The leaders of Communism cannot function without first abandoning every shred of human decency.

That is why there is no higher hilarity or darker irony than the atheist who says that religion has enslaved and killed more people than any other movement. The undisputed title for that goes to atheistic Communism. Its stock in trade is vast concentration camps and raging rivers of blood.

How did Communism take hold in America? It came in a Trojan horse named Progressivism. Progressives wheeled in their agenda over 50 years ago as a "gift" to the oppressed.

The Progressives took control, well, progressively. "Little by little," is the watchword of Communism. The best way to dominate a people and control them utterly is to take away their freedom a little at a time. And to erode rights by a myriad of tiny and almost imperceptible reductions. Death by a thousand cuts. In this way, the people will not see those rights and freedoms being removed until events have passed the point at which these changes can be reversed.

At first, they told us we needed two weeks to flatten the curve of coronavirus. Yet here we are, two years later, and they are still "flattening." Only now, it is not just a virus they are flattening, it is our freedom. Suddenly quacks, drug companies, Facebook, YouTube, and Twitter are the information czars of the Deep State.

They said they wanted to give minorities an even break. Now their theories oppress a new group solely on the basis of their color. That is how you start a race war.

Progressives tell us sexual perversion of every kind must be decriminalized. What they really mean is that moral clarity must be blunted and filed down to a dull edge. Sexual addiction turns decent people into easily manipulated cattle.

Liberalism led to Socialism. Socialism created a swoon. In that stupor, it feels logical to believe you can avoid work and live off the labor of others. Margaret Thatcher explained why Socialism is a pyramid scheme that must fail: "The problem with Socialism is that you eventually run out of other people's money."

Socialism is a gateway drug to Communism—it is the marijuana, if you will, and Communism is the crystal meth. The activist Hollywood stars and Leftie celebrity politicians are your first toke of Communism. Only, you do not know it.

Understand this: they are not using Socialism, race wars, and sexual perversion to go directly to Communism. They are using these things first in order to achieve the next incremental step—chaos. Chaos is the matrix of Marxist Communism. Communists want to trap a nation at its greatest point of desperation. A desperation so deep that the masses willingly accept a totalitarian dictatorship.

They first create a disaster and then lay the blame on the prior culture, the previous administration, and the failed economic system. That is how it's done.

Another way they gain power over you is by manipulating virtue. They create a social reward system that makes you feel righteous about your vegetables, your Prius, and your carbon footprint.

Then viewpoints stiffen into contempt. Now, those who do not recycle, get the jab, or follow the latest virtue signal get cancelled. Suddenly, some lives matter while others do not. Opinions harden into revolutionary convictions. You go from honest debate to snitching on dissenters.

Their number-one weapon is silence. The lyric from the song "The Sound of Silence" says, "'Fools,' said I, 'you do not know, silence like a cancer grows.'" And there is a silence growing in America. And because of that silence, our freedom is dying.

How can anyone looking at us right now say that we look like a free nation? Or that we are still a part of the free world?

A free country can ask questions. We cannot. Our "president" is accountable to no one. He does not have to give us information. We, on the other hand, must provide all of our private information, and we must answer every question—no matter how stupid—that they ask us.

This cancer of silence is not just growing, it is metastasizing. The Left has spread the tumor of censorship into all of our institutions. The Left has recruited soda companies, airlines, banks, universities, and even the NFL to punish free speech. The list of things you cannot say or do without being erased is growing by the hour.

The fact that our culture is silencing us is wicked, but the fact that the American Church is silent is an abomination. The evil is so pervasive that it begs the question, "How can you call yourself a Christian leader and remain silent?"

Silence like a cancer grows. Its tentacles intend to absorb your family. Your silence makes you part of the construction crew that is building a prison for your children and grandchildren. The worst part is that they will live in it without you.

It was in a moment just like this that Dietrich Bonhoeffer begged Germany to listen, but they did not take him seriously. He rebuked the silence of Christians regarding Hitler. He said, "Silence in the face of evil is itself evil: God will not hold us guiltless. Not to speak is to speak. Not to act is to act."

The key factor in America today is that there is still time. Remember, I said that people will not see their rights and freedoms being removed until events have reached the point at which these changes cannot be reversed. Thank God they can still be reversed.

Do not leave quietly. And why should you? Our mighty God has honored you by letting you be born for this hour, for the express purpose of defeating this threat!

# Chapter 4

# IF YOU REMAIN SILENT

*Do not leave quietly*. Those four words possess untold power. First, they are a command to launch the life you were born to live. Second, they are a warning of the perils of remaining silent.

You are at a fork in the road. You must choose wisely. One road leads you to horrendous punishment. The other takes you to untold rewards. That is why leaving quietly is the worst thing you can do.

Mordecai sent a message to Esther that contained another four words that jump off the page:

*"If you remain silent."*

We have heard so much about the danger of speaking out. We are buried under words of advice designed to compel us to mind our own business.

We know all about the dangers of speaking up, but rarely do we consider the cost of remaining silent.

"If you remain silent." Mordecai is telling Esther that disaster is looming. She is a key to preventing the disaster. And finally, disaster will come to *her* if she remains silent.

That is what I am also telling you, dear reader. Disaster is imminent in our nation, and you are a key to averting that disaster.

Here is the entire message to Esther from Mordecai:

> *Do not imagine that you in the king's palace can escape any more than all the Jews. For if you remain silent at this time, liberation and rescue will arise for the Jews from another place, and you and your father's house will perish [since you did not help when you had the chance]. And who knows whether you have attained royalty for such a time as this [and for this very purpose]?* (Esther 4:13-14 AMP)

Here are the specific words of Mordecai to Esther that are the heart of this book:

> *For if you remain silent at this time, liberation and rescue will arise for the Jews from another place, and you and your father's house will perish [since you did not help when you had the chance]* (verse 14 AMP).

He is warning her about what will happen to her if she does not speak to the king. In essence, Mordecai is saying, "Here is what is going to happen if you leave quietly: the life you are trying to protect will be destroyed. The possessions you are hoarding will be taken from you. In short, what you fear the most will come upon you. And the only way to protect everything you love is by facing evil head on and not running from it."

God is saying the same thing to an elite core of American Christians. Esther faced a menace, and now so do we!

What is happening in America is not a conspiracy theory. A puppet president's cognitive decline is being censored from the news. Any story or event that proves that the Leftist-Socialist narrative is a lie is being silenced. When thousands take to the streets to protest tyranny, it is blacked out by the news media. When you speak anything that opposes this Socialist takeover, Facebook and YouTube will ban you. The FBI hunts down parents who speak out against the sexual perversion and racism being taught to their children in classrooms. Those who oppose the vaccination are being fired, shamed, and led away.

Your lukewarm Christian friends tell you that things are not that dire, insisting that "it is all in God's hands." They abuse truth by denying that God needs willing vessels to save people from evil. We the Church are His body. We are His hands and His weapon to destroy the works of the evil one.

Then we hear the tired excuse that, "We should be preaching the Gospel, not politics." Almost always that excuse comes from pastors who have been preaching everything *but* the Gospel.

Suddenly, they are evangelists!

But the true evangelists are the first to call for action against political tyranny. They realize that if freedom dies, we will not be able to preach the Gospel. Andrew Wommack said, "First we must preach the Gospel. Then we must fight to preserve the right to preach the Gospel." (In a later chapter, I will deal directly with the subject of politics in the pulpit.)

But Esther was in no condition to receive this message from Mordecai, because her life was still a fairy tale. And she was in denial. We know this because she was aware of the genocide that Haman planned against the Jews even before Mordecai told her.

Esther 4:4 says this, "When Esther's maids and her eunuchs came and told her [what had happened], the queen was seized by great fear. She sent garments to clothe Mordecai so that he would remove his sackcloth, but he did not accept them" (AMP).

Mordecai is wailing in the streets dressed in sackcloth. But Esther is still in denial and sends nice, clean clothes to Mordecai. She thinks that by dressing him up, it changes the situation. Denial loves outward appearances. I call those clothes "glad rags."

Esther is a wonderful person, but in her current condition she is a threat to her own people. So it is today that we have wonderful preachers with good hearts, but in their current state of denial they are a threat to both the Church and America.

They know what our government is doing to the Church. They know very well the agenda of tyranny that is unfolding in our nation. The lockdowns, masks, forced vaccinations, control of the media, and sponsorship of looters and rioters are all clear to them. But still they persist in preaching sermons that put glad rags on Christians.

Again, I am not talking about bad people. I am referring to good people who are in denial. Yet even a righteous preacher can be poisonous! Proverbs 25:26 says, "Like a muddied fountain and a polluted spring is a righteous man who yields and compromises his integrity before the wicked" (AMP).

It is not the first time in history that this has happened. Wanting to look good in the eyes of an evil culture has been the downfall of many preachers. Charles Spurgeon said, "It is a very ill omen to hear a wicked world clap its hands and shout, 'Well done,' to the Christian man."

Other Christians think declarations of authority, entitlement, and victory exempt them from the war to free our nation. "We'll sit back and just watch God work." This too is denial.

They nurse a myth that Communism cannot happen here. Aleksandr Solzhenitsyn, the famous Russian novelist, said, "There is always this fallacious belief it would not be the same here; here such things are impossible. Alas, all the evil of the twentieth century is possible everywhere on earth."

Not only can Communism happen here, it is happening here. And to deny it is madness.

But we also cling to the subtle and deceptive delusion that it cannot happen here because somehow American Christians are more valuable than Christians in the underground Church.

This tragic mutation of victory and blessing is rooted in defeatism. That is why they never take it to the streets. Much of the Church is like a platoon that has barricaded itself in the barracks and has never gone to war. Why? Because they secretly believe they cannot win. They can only carry on a continuous rehearsal for war.

Why will Esther's punishment be so severe? The next phrase says it, "Since you did not help when you had the chance."

Here is the truth! Of all the reasons God will punish the compromised Christians of America, this one stands out the most: "You did not help when you had the chance."

The Church is crippled by two contradictory doctrines that frame America as either "not needing to be saved from tyranny" or that say, "America is too far gone to be saved." Both extremes are the worst thing to say. They are the natural enemy of reformation and revival.

The Church in Germany, Russia, and China had one thing in common: they did not recognize the threat when they had the chance. They did not act while there was still time.

By the time you read this book, the term *cancel culture* may be passé. I will use it anyway, because satan is using it, *more than anything else*, to destroy our freedom and our witness.

Do not be fooled by the fact that cancel culture seems currently to be more about books, words, and politics. Satan is doing something we see in old movie plots. The husband kills his wife, but also kills two other people chosen at random in order to make it look like there is a serial killer in the neighborhood.

If the Leftists were to openly cancel Christianity, it would be too controversial. So they cancel other things on their way to us. But make no mistake, we are the target, and we have always been the target.

When I wrote the book *Vessels of Fire and Glory*, it was to call a remnant out of the compromised Church. A key verse for the book was 2 Timothy 2:20-21:

> *But in a great house there are not only vessels of gold and silver, but also of wood and clay, some for honor and some for dishonor. Therefore if anyone cleanses himself from the latter, he will be a vessel for honor, sanctified and useful for the Master, prepared for every good work.*

It is a fact that many nations throughout history, when they faced a grave threat, built elite fighting forces. God does that too. *Vessels of Fire and Glory* summoned that elite force out of the great house, the Church, that Paul said had vessels of both honor and dishonor. The promise was that if anyone would separate themselves unto God, they would become vessels of honor, "prepared for every good work."

My goal in that book was to explain that God was drawing a core group into special intimacy with Himself in a way that would unlock strategies to save our nation. They must become an entirely new weapon. But what is that weapon supposed to do, and how is it supposed to do it?

If that book called you *out* of something, then this book is calling you *into* something—the fray!

It was not fair that Esther should have to face such a massive threat. And it is not fair for you, either. But there it is. Shakespeare said, "Some are born great, some achieve greatness, and some have greatness thrust upon them."

And, my dear reader, you are also chosen. You knew this book was not another feel-good treatise about how Daddy God is so into you that He will not lead you into anything uncomfortable.

Sometimes we find a book. Maybe this book found you. And it is telling you that you are not supposed to leave quietly. You are not supposed to check into heaven with a clean uniform, unsoiled by warfare. You are not supposed to be cancelled. You are supposed to make a very special noise. You are supposed to find your voice. And that voice will cancel the works of satan!

# Chapter 5

# THE PANDEMIC IS ONLY THE BEGINNING OF TYRANNY

*So, first of all, let me assert my firm belief that the only thing we have to fear is fear itself—nameless, unreasoning, unjustified terror which paralyzes needed efforts to convert retreat into advance. In every dark hour of our national life, a leadership of frankness and vigor has met with that understanding and support of the people themselves which is essential to victory.*
—Franklin Delano Roosevelt

When a nation's leaders induce fear—nameless, unreasoning, unjustified terror—it paralyzes.

has America in a constant state of retreat. There was so
e could have done about this pandemic that we did not do.
It .. .ld have been over long ago.

It turns out the goal was never to end the virus, but to use it for
other ends. It was to build a system of control. The brilliance of the
great totalitarian leaders of the 1930s was that they kept the public
in a frightened, thoughtless, obedient state while their gangs ran
things into the ground. This is the tactic we are seeing used on us
right now. We have been kept in this condition on purpose.

Nameless, unreasoning, unjustified terror kept us from con-
necting the dots and reading the clues. The evidence of this planned
tyranny was right in front of us. The clues were everywhere.

Mass fear is why we ignored these shocking clues:

- When the churches were locked because we
  were told "public gatherings are dangerous"
  yet mass riots were not only allowed, they were
  encouraged.

- When those who merely asked questions about
  death rates and vaccine side effects faced crushing, instant, vicious punishment and destruction
  of their lives.

- When the very people who paid to create the
  virus are in charge of fighting it, and they make
  the most money from both the virus and the cure.

- When shutting down the schools was the worst
  form of child abuse America has ever seen.

- When new strains of the virus conveniently
  appear just in time to extend their state of

emergency. An extension required because their mechanism of control is taking longer to build than they thought.

In the meantime, they have made significant headway. They saw how they can get millions of people to believe lies and do ridiculous things. You have seen it too. The whole world has seen it. Billions of people acting strangely compliant. Taking orders without thinking or, in the majority of cases, even seriously investigating what they have been told.

They willingly and unquestioningly accepted the vaccines (if they are vaccines), wore masks, and lived obediently under lockdowns. *We are watching the largest group of conformists in world history.*

Roger L. Simon, award-winning novelist and Oscar-nominated screenwriter, said, "We live in a culture of pervasive obedience; what has recently been called mass formation psychosis, but you don't need a fancy term to see it. It's everywhere, people giving up their personal agency, even their ability to reason, out of fear and willingly adhering to the mass."[1]

But nothing tells us the state of affairs more than this: there was a workable plan to end the pandemic that was buried, silenced, and ignored. The tyranny is so pervasive that it does not matter how much credibility or expertise a doctor or scientist has, they are attacked and labeled as quacks and liars.

Roger L. Simon did an important poll.

In a personal survey of those who have most willingly and unquestionably accepted the vaccines (if that's what they are), worn masks, and lived obediently under lockdowns as if that were the only way to survive, I have met absolutely none who have read the works of Robert F. Kennedy, Jr., Alex Berenson, or Dr. Scott Atlas or heard the lectures or seen the readily available videos by the likes of Drs. Robert Malone, Peter McCullough, Harvey Risch, or Vladimir Zelenko, not to mention many others, including the august group that signed the Great Barrington Declaration. Many don't even know what it is or even that it exists. They certainly haven't read the statement, although it's only a few pages.

That's right, none. Zero. Even though, in the case of the books, the works of the first three authors are best-sellers. And, yes, they may have seen them bashed on CNN or some other "reliable scientific source." But that's about it. Read for themselves? Why do that when they are told it's nonsense?[2]

Who is doing all of this to us? China, along with the ruling-class elite, which includes the multinational corporate network. We have the same familiar faces: Soros, the Clintons, and the Obamas.

They are now joined by the new elites—the current tech-billionaires club, in which Fauci and Biden are just hollowed-out imps in their grand scheme. Their goal is to unleash tyranny on a scale we have never seen before.

But this is only the beginning. The next stage is to foment hatred against the unvaccinated. Without this hatred, they cannot reach their next benchmark of control. I believe we are being programmed to hate the unvaccinated in the same way that Hitler programmed Germany to hate Jews.

I could never understand how a civilized and cultured society such as Germany could have committed such barbaric atrocities as concentration camps, gas chambers, and mass extermination of people—even children. We are talking about a modern nation filled with civilized and highly educated people. How could they plunge into such extraordinary evil?

*Now I know how.*

I know how because I have watched hatred grow day by day. I have watched the drip, drip, drip of tyranny. Already, 29 percent of Democrats favor putting the unvaccinated in camps; 19 percent believe the unvaccinated should have their children taken away.

They want vaccination passports to lead to registering and marking the unvaccinated. A majority of Democrat voters favor fines on the unvaccinated.

Meanwhile, the hostility grows. In a New York City school, a young girl was kept outside for hours in freezing weather because she was not "vaxed." Another girl was locked in a hot library for four hours. The Ronald MacDonald House for Children evicted a four-year-old with leukemia, along with his family, because they refused to take the jab. And many potential transplant patients have been taken off the list because they would not submit to the tyranny of forced vaccination.

Our foes wield astonishing power. They have mountains of money, unlimited connections, and enormous influence. Will they destroy nations and borders? Will they drive the Church underground? Is it possible that they can indeed plow under the entire moral foundation of America, and even the world?

They are on schedule for world domination. But there is good news for those who will follow God into battle against this tyranny.

So, you ask, "What is God doing?" God is laughing. He is laughing at their plans. Psalm 2, in verse 4, states, "He who sits in the heavens shall laugh; the Lord shall hold them in derision." God laughs and mocks their plans. He heaps divine ridicule on them.

But God's dealings do not stop there. In verse 5 it says, "Then He shall speak to them in His wrath, and distress them in His deep displeasure." God is not only laughing at their plans—He will wreck their plans. His wrath will be poured out on their vain imaginings.

The word *backfire* does not *begin* to cover the next act of God. *If God's army acts, God will act against men who try to bury the Church and set up their own kingdom.* The nations are the express inheritance of Jesus Christ. Psalm 2 goes on to state in verses 7-8, "The Lord has said to Me, 'You are My Son, today I have begotten You. Ask of Me, and I will give You the nations for Your inheritance, and the ends of the earth for Your possession.'"

Where this ends hinges mostly on you and me. If we remain silent. if we leave quietly, then they have already destroyed us and our families. It is time to expose them. It is time to ignore those things that appear to be impossible and follow God into battle. He has plans to destroy their plans, and His plans depend on our participation.

## Notes

1. Roger L. Simon, "How My View of the Holocaust Was Altered During COVID," The Epoch Times, January 31, 2022, https://www.theepochtimes.com/how-my-view-of-the -holocaust-was-altered-during-covid_4247128.html.
2. Ibid.

Chapter 6

# FIFTY MILLION HAND GRENADES

*You and I have a rendezvous with destiny. We will preserve for our children this, the last best hope of man on earth, or we will sentence them to take the first step into a thousand years of darkness. If we fail, at least let our children and our children's children say of us we justified our brief moment here. We did all that could be done.*
—RONALD REAGAN

JUST AS THE UNITED STATES WAS CRAWLING OUT OF THE Great Depression, Germany started World War II in Europe and Japan attacked Pearl Harbor. The United States now needed to build a vast war machine.

President Franklin Roosevelt had no choice but to convince massive corporations like DuPont, General Motors, Ford Motors,

Boeing, and Kaiser to build the arsenal of Democracy to save the free world. The problem was that Roosevelt had made avowed enemies of the men who led these companies.

He won the presidency by promising to expose their corruption. He smeared them in his campaign speeches and provoked Congress to investigate them. How would he get them to set aside this feud in order to save humanity?

Roosevelt did it by painting one simple, clear picture of reality: if these men did not act, Germany and Japan would win. Pierre DuPont, William Boeing, Henry Ford, and Henry J. Kaiser would have no companies, and their money would do nothing to protect their children and grandchildren.

But Roosevelt had a second daunting task to perform. He needed to now impress upon these powerful men what it would take to win. So he ordered the military to combine all of their skills to assess the threat, design a strategy, and calculate what they needed to build. What kinds of weapons were needed? How many of them did we need?

Pierre DuPont was one of the first to obey the order to meet with Army scientists. They handed him a sample of a new hand grenade the military wanted him to make. He asked, "How many do you need?" They replied, "We need fifty million." Fifty million hand grenades! In that paralyzing moment, DuPont finally realized how gigantic the effort must be to save the free world.

For the Church in America, the "fifty million hand grenades" moment has arrived. Our enemy is every bit as large and as lethal today as Nazi Germany and Imperialist Japan were then. Only this time we are like that horror movie. You know the one where they discovered that the threatening phone calls were coming from inside the house.

Our fifty million hand grenades moment means that Christian leaders must immediately drop their offenses with each other. They must let go of division and bitterness and find common ground in order to save the nation from a thousand years of darkness. They must act as a single unit. They must build a "revival war machine" to save American freedom.

Not only that, but the Holy Spirit is at work doing to the Church what Roosevelt did with these corporate titans. He is showing us what is at stake. His voice is crying out to everyone, from celebrity pastors to Christian billionaires to everyday believers. He is ordering us to toss aside petty squabbles and build the movement that can destroy the present threat to our way of life.

## HERE IS WHAT IS AT STAKE

Fact: The leaders of wokeness, Socialism, and Critical Race Theory will stop at nothing to destroy our nation. We must destroy the threat, or the threat will destroy us. It is as simple as that.

Victor Davis Hanson said, "So this is a revolutionary Jacobin movement. I think everybody saw that in 2021, and I think they fear rightly that it's going to continue in 2022—even if it explodes and takes us with it. But they're not going to change on their own."[1]

Fact: No nation has ever lost two generations in a row and survived. We have already lost one.

Fact: The second and last generation is under a withering assault by the most sophisticated, anti-God manipulation technology the world has ever seen.

Fact: No modern nation that has lost freedom has ever regained it.

Fact: The children of freedom are blindly drifting toward the vilest system of government the world has ever known. And the Church is the only one who can stop it. But right now she is drowsy, divided, and convinced that "it can't happen here."

In their day, DuPont, Ford, Boeing, and Kaiser got the message. Not only did they make the 50 million hand grenades, they launched over 6,000 ships, building about 7 per day. Henry Ford's workers at Willow Run built a staggering 8,685 B-24 bombers— at the astonishing rate of one per hour.

Now we must get the message from our field commander— the Holy Spirit. The Holy Spirit's work never changes. His process of taking raw material and making a living, breathing conduit of His power has never changed. In 2,000 years, it has not been shortened or compromised one iota.

You were chosen. You are destined to confront evil. You have no option. I want this book to push the pause button on your life. I need you to see the drastic and colossal action we must undertake to save our nation. We cannot talk about what we *want* to do or about what we *think* we can do. Our cry must be, "Whatever it takes!"

Jesus sent the Holy Spirit for this very kind of threat. The Spirit of God is the commander in chief of Christian endeavors on earth. Everything He does leads to victory. He is the chief reason that the gates of hell will not prevail against the Church.

We cannot do what we know we must do without a divine plan. In the next chapter we get our first glimpse. We are about to see a model for turning impossible situations around, through determined resistance to satan.

## NOTE

1. Victor Davis Hanson, "Democrats are 'revolutionaries' pushing radical agenda 'even if it explodes,'" Fox News, December 31, 2021, https://www.foxnews.com/media/victor-davis -hanson-democrats-revolutionaries-radical-agenda-ingraham -angle.

# Chapter 7

# THEY TOLD ME TO QUIT WHEN I DECIDED NOT TO LEAVE QUIETLY

I WAS TOLD TO QUIT. THE PERSON WHO SAID THIS WAS deeply concerned about my welfare. They made a chilling case for me to go silent while there was still time. They told me that anything I might say would be twisted—and that not only would I be banned, but they would go after me until they had destroyed my career as a preacher.

But because the Holy Spirit had warned me in advance that they were coming, I was ready to answer this person. So now I am going to relate to you what God told me about quitting. God gave me these verses:

> *Now the Lord spoke to Paul in the night by a vision,*
> *"Do not be afraid, but speak, and do not keep silent;*
> *for I am with you, and no one will attack you to hurt*
> *you; for I have many people in this city." And he* [Paul]

*continued there a year and six months, teaching the word of God among them* (Acts 18:9-11).

The fact is that this this ministry can't be explained in the natural anyway. It was born supernaturally, and it will be sustained supernaturally.

Instead, I have decided not to leave quietly. Not only am I not quitting, I will amplify all the words I receive from the Lord. This book is my personal act of defiance.

God stands ready to refresh and empower you for a fresh attack on evil.

*But those who wait on the Lord shall renew their strength; they shall mount up with wings like eagles, they shall run and not be weary, they shall walk and not faint* (Isaiah 40:31).

Now, I want to speak heart to heart with the remnant of God in America—*this is a test*. And we are in the worst part of that test. The rage of anti-God social media is out of control, because they feel emboldened to do whatever they want, and because they think Trump is done and that he is gone for good.

They are raining down shame and accusation on anyone who speaks truth. Nevertheless, we must not fear and we must not fold. Those preachers who cave in to fear and then abandon their message will pay a heavy price—not only from shame, but also from regret—because they gave up just before the breakthrough.

*For it is the time [destined] for judgment to begin with the household of God; and if it begins with us, what*

will the outcome be for those who do not respect or
believe or obey the gospel of God? (1 Peter 4:17 AMP)

*Evil is having its day.*

You knew this wasn't going to be easy. You knew their
evil had to have its day. You also knew there was no way we
could have challenged these devils without unleashing a storm
of hatred.

I know that fear can feel irresistible in this storm. I know it is
disheartening when you see people you respected—and some of
the last people you would have imagined—caving in and recanting
their convictions.

But again, *this is the worst time to fold.* This is the worst time to
doubt what God has said to you. *Fear is not an option.*

Compromising with the enemy can be seductive, but it will end
in disaster, and, as I said, you will feel deep remorse if the breakthrough comes right after you quit. Can you imagine having to live
with that for the rest of your life?

> *But He knows the way that I take; when He has tested
> me, I shall come forth as gold* (Job 23:10).

*I feel God is imploring us to hang on a little longer.* I know how
hard it has been! You have heard stories that promised to uncover
the truth and turn the tide. Each time they raised our hopes, and
when it didn't happen it wounded us.

I am not asking you to trust in myths, legends, or conspiracy
theories. I am compelling you to trust in God Himself and in His
inspired words recorded in the Bible.

*Please. Just hang in there.* The enemy is going to be shocked! Hang in there. There are options we don't know about. God is going to finish what He started in our great movement!

> *Therefore do not cast away your confidence, which has great reward. For you have need of endurance, so that after you have done the will of God, you may receive the promise: "For yet a little while, and He who is coming will come and will not tarry. Now the just shall live by faith; but if anyone draws back, My soul has no pleasure in him." But we are not of those who draw back to perdition, but of those who believe to the saving of the soul* (Hebrews 10:35-39).

# Chapter 8

# FIVE THINGS THAT SILENCE WILL DO TO YOUR MINISTRY

*Silence in the face of evil is itself evil: God will not hold us guiltless. Not to speak is to speak. Not to act is to act.*
—DIETRICH BONHOEFFER

"I KEEP POLITICS OUT OF THE PULPIT." I AM GOING TO WRITE about the five devastating things an excuse like that will do to your ministry. We have spent so much time talking about the hazards of speaking out that we have not realized the disasters of remaining silent. The nation is careening toward new levels of division that are more intense than what we see now. Be warned! The middle ground is going to disappear, and soon.

This message is urgent. But it is not about bashing pastors. It is my honor to work with thousands of sincere men and women of God who are in our pulpits.

Sadly, there are also many other preachers who have been hoodwinked by the devil. They think they are doing the right thing by remaining silent on burning issues. It is the deep desire of my heart for this book to warn those preachers about the disaster that will come to any preacher who refuses to stand against evil, when the evil is so glaring and the price of disobedience is so high.

*It is wrong to keep politics out of the pulpit for the simple reason that it is no longer about politics—it is about evil.*

I believe there are only two reasons that the subject of politics is being kept out of the pulpit: preachers do not believe tyranny is about to destroy our freedom, or they are so controlled by fear that they are in denial that it is tyranny.

No matter what, the tyranny is here and the Bible is clear about preaching in this season. Here are five disasters that will befall preachers who continue to hide behind a lame excuse:

## 1. Many in your congregation believe you no longer care about them.

They are being fired for refusing the vaccine or simply because they are Christians. Their children are suffering at school—being expelled for wearing Christian T-shirts, being groomed by teachers for sexual perversion, being labelled racist oppressors by Critical Race Theory. They are facing brutal things every day. If you do not address, equip, or defend them in the war that is being waged against their families, they will take their family to a pastor who *will* stand up for them. The sheep want help. They need help. Paul said, "I kept back nothing that was helpful" (Acts 20:20).

When Christian moms go to school board meetings to confront child porn in the classroom, they look around and wonder, "Where is my pastor?"

## 2. *You are ignoring your duty and your power to stop persecution of the Church.*

Paul models this duty for you in Acts 16:37-38:

> *But Paul said to them, "They have beaten us openly, uncondemned Romans, and have thrown us into prison. And now do they put us out secretly? No indeed! Let them come themselves and get us out." And the officers told these words to the magistrates, and they were afraid when they heard that they were Romans.*

Paul did not do this to protect himself. He did it to protect the fledgling church at Philippi from rogue government.

## 3. *God will seek a replacement.*

You are not only disappointing your people, you are grieving God. Mordecai delivered this warning to Esther:

> *For if you remain completely silent at this time, relief and deliverance will arise for the Jews from another place, but you and your father's house will perish. Yet who knows whether you have come to the kingdom for such a time as this?* (Esther 4:14)

Likewise, God gave *you* a pulpit and influence "for such a time as this."

## 4. Government will not allow you to remain neutral.

> *But Peter and John answered and said to them, "Whether it is right in the sight of God to listen to you more than to God, you judge. For we cannot but speak the things which we have seen and heard"* (Acts 4:19-20).

Peter realized that he had no choice but to resist the irrational ban on the Gospel. He knew that, left unchallenged, their restrictions would lead to control over everything they preached.

*In the great global reset, the state will hand you your sermon topics.* In the short term, if you remain silent, they will let you keep "woke" members, but in the long term, you can lose everything.

## 5. You are also endangering the souls of believers who consider themselves woke.

Yes, there are many who see nothing wrong with combining Christ and wokeness. They don't see the danger because they are blind.

Denial will keep you from facing that wokeness and Christianity cannot mix. Wokeness and the Democrat Party no longer just support abortion, they celebrate it. They no longer advocate for transgender rights, they are trying to destroy anyone who disagrees with their sexual mandates. They no longer just disagree with the Bible and Christianity, they seek to eradicate both. Wokeness hates everything a Christian stands for. If "woke Christians" in your church do not realize that they cannot be "woke" *and* Christian—that is a reflection on your preaching.

*You should be more concerned about their souls than their membership.*

You may have held on to them physically, but they have already left the Church spiritually. Worst of all, they do not know that the empty shell of Christianity they cling to will not save them.

In conclusion: I see no upside to staying neutral and quiet. I see only disaster. In fact, I will probably not have to write on this subject again, because the idea of remaining quiet about evil will very soon collapse under the weight of its own folly.

There is still great hope for every ministry that chooses to sacrifice for the truth. Our ministry is seeing great fire and harvest. Before it is too late, follow Paul's exhortation to Timothy, "Preach the word! Be ready in season and out of season. Convince, rebuke, exhort, with all longsuffering and teaching" (2 Tim. 4:2).

Chapter 9

# How "Woke Christians" Leave Quietly

*First of all, let me remind you: being a "woke Christian" is as impossible as being a godly atheist.*

"Wokeness" begins with platitudes about race, justice, and equality. Going from that to hard facts, fairness, and a workable plan seems to elude the "woke folk." When pinned down to practical solutions, their brain drain is often instant and they begin to ramble and say things that make no sense in the real world. The sure sign that you are a Leftist is that you confuse feeling with thinking.

That two-step transition from ranting to incoherence is perfectly embodied in Alexandria Ocasio Cortez. Watch her work. She begins, as I just said, with tirades against evil. After that, it is grim, indeed. She simply makes no sense.

As Scott Moorefield said, "Just about everything that comes out of the young congresswoman-elect's mouth is either patently untrue, ridiculously unworkable, unintentionally hilarious, or ripped straight from the pages of Das Kapital (in which case, it's all of the above)."[1]

She compared global warming to World War II. She said, "The last time we had a really major existential threat in this country was around World War II. So, we've been here before, and we have a blueprint of what we did before. None of these things are new ideas. What we had was an existential threat in the context of a war, and what we did was that we chose to mobilize and industrialize our entire economy and we put hundreds of thousands if not millions of people to work in defending our shores and defending this country."[2]

Doesn't everyone immediately think, "Hey, let's do to global warming what we did to the Nazis?"

The same mental drain occurs when you question the "woke Christian" (if they let you). They begin by representing the Left as being more like the organic message of Jesus in that they imply, "We care for the poor and fight for justice for the disenfranchised."

Those on the Left do not care for the poor. The gifts to charity by the Obamas, Clintons, and Bidens are piddling. Conservative Christian organizations care for the poor with staggering generosity.

Wokeness is more concerned with slogans and the *appearance* of caring. And some of their priorities are mind numbing.

Franklin Graham set up a large tent hospital in Central Park to help handle the massive shortage of hospital beds. New York City ordered him to pack up and leave because of—are you ready for this—his view of biblical morality.

Sometimes, the level of absurdity of a "woke" Christian is hilarious. A pastor of a Spirit-filled denomination in California defended the idea that Jesus was "woke." He said that Jesus was asleep in the boat and the disciples woke Him. Therefore, He is "woke."

When you even say the words *woke Christian*, it is the worst form of silence there is. You are talking, but not saying anything.

Ask them this: "Do you believe the Bible is the complete and inerrant Word of God?" Watch closely what happens next. They either do not know what the Bible says, or they do know but do not believe the Bible is God-breathed.

Taking directly from what "woke Christians" have claimed to believe, here is a list of the ways "wokeness" clashes with the Bible.

- Biblical marriage can only be between a man and a woman, because the Bible recognizes only male and female genders. "He created them male and female, and blessed them and called them Mankind in the day they were created" (Gen. 5:2).

- The Bible states that human life begins in the womb, thus making abortion murder. "For he will be great in the sight of the Lord, and shall drink neither wine nor strong drink. He will also be filled with the Holy Spirit, even from his mother's womb" (Luke 1:15).

- The Bible's definition of love makes it racism to hate, censor, or refuse education or employment to anyone because of their color, and that includes white people. "There is neither Jew nor Greek, there is neither slave nor free, there is

- neither male nor female; for you are all one in Christ Jesus" (Gal. 3:28).
- The Bible says Christ is the only way to salvation, so you cannot mix Christ and Islam. "Jesus said to him, 'I am the way, the truth, and the life. No one comes to the Father except through Me'" (John 14:6).
- The Bible says that if you do not take care of your own family first, you are worse than an infidel and have denied the faith. Open borders do not help those coming to this country illegally. On the contrary, that policy has sent many children into sexual slavery.

But the way it does damage to your family is this: it permits criminals to roam your streets undocumented and possibly infected with a new strain of COVID. And a flood of deadly Fentanyl has poured into this nation since woke Leftists scrapped Trump's border policies. This is not only irresponsible but, according to the Bible, a sin against your own family. "But if anyone does not provide for his own, and especially for those of his household, he has denied the faith and is worse than an unbeliever" (1 Tim. 5:8).

"Woke Christians," if they do answer the question of the Bible's divine inspiration, will often answer by deflecting—that is, they will quote other scriptures (always out of context) in order to try to cancel the ones they do not agree with. The Bible must be taken as a whole, or not at all.

And that, by the way, is another thing the Bible teaches. "All Scripture is given by inspiration of God, and is profitable for doctrine, for reproof, for correction, for instruction in righteousness" (2 Tim. 3:16).

Still, others will say that you can be Christian and not believe in the Bible. This is utter madness because it turns the central authority away from God and His Word and places it on subjective human feelings. So now, you can call yourself a Christian and believe in anything. This is the same credo that drives the transgender movement. All you have to say is, "I self-identify...."

Placing feelings over facts is not just rebellion against truth, it places trust in an extremely unreliable and wicked thing—the human heart. "The heart is deceitful above all things, and desperately wicked; who can know it?" (Jer. 17:9).

The Bible instructs us to meet together and to resist government lockdowns based on our faith (see Heb. 10:25; Acts 4:19).

The "woke Christian" is agreeing to policies that are anti-Bible, and is agreeing with people who hate the Bible and who are at war with the Church.

> *Do not be unequally bound together with unbelievers [do not make mismatched alliances with them, inconsistent with your faith]. For what partnership can righteousness have with lawlessness? Or what fellowship can light have with darkness? What harmony can there be between Christ and Belial (Satan)? Or what does a believer have in common with an unbeliever? What agreement is there between the temple of God and idols? For we are the temple of the living God; just as God said: "I will dwell among them and walk among them; and I will be their God, and they shall be My people"* (2 Corinthians 6:14-16 AMP).

Here is one way that wokeness corresponds to circumcision: Paul wrote in Galatians 5:2, "Indeed I, Paul, say to you that if you become circumcised, Christ will profit you nothing." In the same way, embracing an anti-Christian belief system separates you from Christ.

If "woke Christians" cannot answer the question about the authority of the Bible, likewise, they will not be able to answer this question: "How can you support an agenda that is unambiguously anti-Christ and then call yourself a Christian?"

## Notes

1. Scott Moorefield, "The Seven Craziest Things Alexandria Ocasio-Cortez Has Said So Far," Townhall, November 26, 2018, https://townhall.com/columnists/ scottmorefield/2018/11/26/the-seven-craziest-things -alexandria-ocasiocortez-has-said-so-far-n2536456.

2. Ibid.

# Chapter 10

# DO NOT LEAVE QUIETLY

THIS CHAPTER WILL TELL YOU WHAT THIS BOOK IS ABOUT. Let's look at how Paul the apostle responded in a life and death moment when, had he left quietly, he could have destroyed thousands of lives in a city. And he could have destroyed a miracle for all the ages.

He chose not to leave quietly in a situation that is exactly the same as the situation we face today. It is eerie how it matches what is happening in our nation. This chapter will leave no doubt about the choice you must make—and how to make it.

Paul had just cast a devil of divination out of a fortune-telling girl in Philippi. Her owners flew into a rage when they could no longer exploit her. It all takes place in Act 16:

> *And they brought them to the magistrates, and said,*
> *"These men, being Jews, exceedingly trouble our*
> *city; and they teach customs which are not lawful*
> *for us, being Romans, to receive or observe." Then*
> *the multitude rose up together against them; and the*

*magistrates tore off their clothes and commanded them to be beaten with rods. And when they had laid many stripes on them, they threw them into prison, commanding the jailer to keep them securely. Having received such a charge, he put them into the inner prison and fastened their feet in the stocks.*

*But at midnight Paul and Silas were praying and singing hymns to God, and the prisoners were listening to them. Suddenly there was a great earthquake, so that the foundations of the prison were shaken; and immediately all the doors were opened and everyone's chains were loosed. And the keeper of the prison, awaking from sleep and seeing the prison doors open, supposing the prisoners had fled, drew his sword and was about to kill himself. But Paul called with a loud voice, saying, "Do yourself no harm, for we are all here."*

*Then he called for a light, ran in, and fell down trembling before Paul and Silas. And he brought them out and said, "Sirs, what must I do to be saved?"*

*So, they said, "Believe on the Lord Jesus Christ, and you will be saved, you and your household." Then they spoke the word of the Lord to him and to all who were in his house. And he took them the same hour of the night and washed their stripes. And immediately he and all his family were baptized.*

*Now when he had brought them into his house, he set food before them; and he rejoiced, having believed in God with all his household. And when it was day, the magistrates sent the officers, saying, "Let those men go." So, the keeper of the prison reported these words to Paul, saying, "The magistrates have sent to let you go. Now therefore depart, and go in peace."*

*But Paul said to them, "They have beaten us openly, uncondemned Romans, and have thrown us into prison. And now do they put us out secretly? No indeed! Let them come themselves and get us out." And the officers told these words to the magistrates, and they were afraid when they heard that they were Romans. Then they came and pleaded with them and brought them out, and asked them to depart from the city. So, they went out of the prison and entered the house of Lydia; and when they had seen the brethren, they encouraged them and departed* (Acts 16:20-40).

# THERE ARE FIVE FACTORS IN THIS STORY

## *1. Mob rule—evil, greedy men and crooked leaders lie about the law and raise a mob.*

To foment rage, they raised a mob. And that is what is happening in America. "Black Lives Matter" is a phrase I agree with, but the organization is now Marxist, approves of violence, and collects untold millions of dollars without any accountability. Big Pharma used mob mentality to sell vast amounts of their vaccines. Democrats eager to stay in power have weaponized Antifa, backed mobs, and inflamed false investigations. Mobs have used tyranny to force the LGBTQ agenda on our children. There are many more examples of how greed has created mobs and false laws.

Legacy media and social media censor any information that opposes the mob rule. A national blackout of information is guaranteeing they remain in control of the masses. And they are creating illegal laws.

The men described in Acts 16 invented a law when they said, "They teach customs which are not lawful for us, being Romans, to receive or observe" in order to justify beating and arresting Paul and Silas. That is exactly what we see today. Mob rule and the satanic spirit of lawlessness have created illegal laws, church and business lockdowns, riots, road blocks, mask mandates, vaccine mandates, etc.

## 2. *In prison, Paul and Silas sang praises at midnight.*

Wounded and chained, they sang praises to God. Paul kept his heart strong. He demonstrated by his worship that he trusted God, honored God, and expected a miracle.

Instead of singing at midnight, many Christian leaders collapsed beneath the stress and demands of the pandemic. They closed their doors. They parroted woke terminology in lame Zoom calls from the ease of their living rooms, while the faithful remnant across our nation stood strong and waited for the prison doors to open.

## 3. *Paul discerned the true purpose of the earthquake.*

Suddenly, God destroyed the jail with a strange earthquake. The quake collapsed the entire building, but no one was hurt. The cell doors flew open, and the chains fell off the prisoners.

That is precisely what is happening right now in America. An earthquake has come. The walls of the prison are collapsing. Leftists are losing their grip on us. The secret deeds of the Wuhan lab, Pfizer, Fauci, Biden, YouTube, Facebook, and so many more can now be seen in the rubble.

Paul knows that God has used this earthquake to make an emphatic statement. That is what I am after—an emphatic statement. I want God to speak to you with the force of an earthquake. I want His Word to you to go off the Richter scale.

Paul the apostle waited for clarity about what he was supposed to do next, just as these earthquakes have opened the door for me to do something.

Paul might have just skipped town the moment the jail blew open. He could have even boasted at the next town how God sent the earthquake to save him. Yet he knew that this miracle was not for private use but for a much deeper purpose than self-preservation.

Safety and self-preservation are the bane of modern Christians. It is astounding how much some Christian organizations will compromise, just to survive. And how much they will adulterate their message and mission for personal safety.

Paul felt compelled to stay, and he was about to find out why.

## 4. *Paul got angry.*

They asked Paul to leave quietly. They wanted to keep their crimes a secret. But Paul said, "They have beaten us openly, uncondemned Romans, and have thrown us into prison. And now do they put us out secretly? No indeed! Let them come themselves and get us out." Paul was no longer just a preacher—he was a freedom fighter.

*Commanding politicians is the new role of God's remnant in America*. Paul knew that their laws violated Roman law. He also knew that Roman officials did not tolerate pinhead rogue rulers who arbitrarily cast aside the laws of Rome.

Paul was modeling Christian civil disobedience against rogue government. And he was doing it for big reasons. What Paul did to them is what God is asking us to do against church lockdowns. Forced vaccinations. Critical Race Theory and LGBTQ curriculum overruling parents. What do they all have in common? They violate the Constitution of the United States.

The false application of Romans 13 is no longer an excuse. Romans 13:3 says, "For rulers are not a terror to good works, but to evil. Do you want to be unafraid of the authority? Do what is good, and you will have praise from the same." If government is a terror to good works—that is not the government we submit to. Moreover, by disobeying Philippian law, Paul was obeying Roman law.

But the biggest reason Paul had to act was that he knew satan was behind all of this. Paul could see what satan was doing. Satan wanted to destroy the newly created Philippian church, so he had Paul arrested. Paul understood that if he did not act to protect the young church against evil government, it would be open season on these new converts. At stake also was the very creation of the Book of Philippians.

That should speak loudly to those pastors who believe they should stay out of politics. Because it is quite likely that they are not only in covenant with Leftists by default, but also with satan.

And, if God is doing a miracle to preserve the Church's freedom, then Christian leaders should stand their ground.

Paul got mad and then he got busy.

### 5. *Paul enforced the miracle.*

*First, he openly confronted them with the crimes they had committed and the laws they had broken.* "They have beaten us openly, uncondemned Romans, and have thrown us into prison" (vs. 37a). That is what every believer must do. Speak up! Speak out! Expose the criminal behavior of those in power.

Next, Paul was saying, "*You are not going to get away with this.*" "And now do they put us out secretly?" (vs. 37b). Every day people are doing this! There is nothing more compelling than the video of a mom railing against evil in a schoolboard meeting—exposing the sexual perversion that is being taught in classrooms filled with five-year-olds. Because she loves her child, she will not leave quietly. And because it has all been recorded on video, the evil being perpetrated by the schoolboard is defeated.

Finally, Paul *took authority and demanded action.* "No indeed! Let them come themselves and get us out" (vs. 37c). He could never have done this without knowing his rights. He knew Roman law. He knew the Romans and what they would do to those officials if they found out what they had done.

*By staying, Paul unleashed amazing authority to encourage and protect the freedom of the Church.* The magistrates were compelled, not only to march alongside Paul, but they also made an epic stop at the house church in Philippi. Paul was putting evil in its place, and at the same time strengthening the children of God. "So, they went out of the prison and entered the house of Lydia; and when they had seen the brethren, they encouraged them and departed" (vs. 40). Paul put the welfare of the people of God above his own safety.

*Do not leave quietly!* Not now! Not ever! We have every reason not to give up. There is still so much hope for our nation. We can still raise a roar and see stunning results. Instead of defeating us, the enemy will be stunned and rendered powerless by the words and the actions that explode from within us. You have too many promises of victory to turn back now.

How could Paul have imagined the way it was going to turn out and how drastically the situation would turn in his favor? Could he have imagined an earthquake? Or that his oppressors would submit to his demands?

Here is what Paul said about yet another imprisonment he faced, "I want to report to you, friends, that my imprisonment here has had the opposite of its intended effect. Instead of being squelched, the Message has actually prospered" (Phil. 1:12 MSG).

God can reverse satan's intended effect on our land—but only if we do not leave quietly.

Section Two

WHAT IT WILL TAKE

# Chapter 11

# GOD IS GIVING YOU PERMISSION TO SAVE AMERICA

*Will God ever ask you to do something you are not able to do? The answer is, yes—all the time! It must be that way, for God's glory and Kingdom. If we function according to our ability alone, we get the glory; if we function according to the power of the Spirit within us, God gets the glory. He wants to reveal Himself to a watching world.*
—HENRY BLACKABY

## PERMISSION TO SAVE AMERICA

I want to introduce you to the next section of this book. Here, we will shake up the sense of inadequacy and the sense of impossibility. Here, we will take our first steps toward making a massive noise before we leave.

These days, the warrior of God can be vexed with discouragement. They can feel crushed between the two jaws of a vise. One jaw is the blatant depravity of our "woke" culture. The other jaw is the disheartening cowardice of preachers. These factors weigh you down, steal your joy, and even crush your spirit.

The Christian warrior sees what is happening in our culture:

Our government calls Christian moms "domestic terrorists" for trying to protect and defend their children from schoolboards with a woke agenda who are bent on promoting Critical Race Theory and perversion.

Then there are the bands of organized thugs who are systematically robbing high-end stores.

And the Leftist governors who allow drugstores to be looted on a daily basis by the homeless, with no consequences.

The Bible tells us about the vexation of Lot in Sodom. "For that just man, while living among them, felt his righteous soul tormented day after day by what he saw and heard of their lawless acts" (2 Pet. 2:8 AMP). This is exactly what the core of God's people are feeling in our culture.

Now, look at what continues to happen in our pulpits:

The nation is on fire. As I have said repeatedly, the pandemic lockdown set the mechanism in place to silence the Church. Most Christians believe our government is hostile to our faith. Yet pastors who have the influence to push back against tyranny refuse to do so—even though they know the flocks they are supposed to be shepherding are suffering under the lash of persecution and perversion.

Many pastors confuse politics with evil. It is no longer politics. We are now confronting pure evil.

One megachurch pastor in Colorado said, from the pulpit, that he has decided not to talk about politics from the pulpit because lifelong friends "are no longer in our lives, just because they disagreed with us over *politics, or some silly thing!*" He said, "If I were to bring up some political idea today, I guarantee there would be 40 different opinions and 400 emails. I've tried it before and that's what I get."

Friends and emails? Is that all it takes to neutralize this man? Imagine how that statement sounds to the martyrs from centuries past and to today's suffering underground Church?

The warrior of God is opposed from the front and betrayed from behind. No wonder freedom fighters of faith can feel totally drained.

Why is there so little preaching about actually taking ground back from the devil? What can we do about the demons that are strangling America? Can we dismantle their ramparts? They have brought bitter division, mass addiction, and total deception. Can we stop them? Not only can we, it is our sworn duty to tear them down.

The Bible says, "For the weapons of our warfare are not carnal but mighty in God for pulling down strongholds, casting down arguments and every high thing that exalts itself against the knowledge of God" (2 Cor. 10:4-5).

The Bible says we can "cast down every high thing." Most preaching and teaching today leaves the impression that there is very little we can do. But that begs a question:

If we can't tear down strongholds, isn't God guilty of child abuse on a grand scale? He is guilty of letting Paul awaken a deep hope that can never be fulfilled. The whole point of 2 Corinthians

10:4-5 was to provoke the Church to take up the mighty weapons of God.

Likewise, there are two elements in the modern Church that must silence the message of victory over demons in order for those churches to stay in business. The two elements are the "therapeutic" church and the "gloom and doom" church.

The therapeutic church must focus on happy talk and self-fulfillment. Shaking up their comfort zones with talk of warfare threatens their attendance numbers. To survive, they must distract Christians to be satisfied with lesser goals and lower living. They are guilty of unwittingly helping the devil to keep the Army of God powerless.

Gloom and doom preachers keep the Church on the defensive by telling them to take cover. Fear sells books and conspiracy theories sell survival, not revival. Gloom and doom prophets—like good Democrats—must cheer for global domination, global warming, and global disasters to keep Christians buying. They do not equip you to confront and conquer evil because they don't believe it's possible.

God has chosen to act in answer to prayer. He waits until His people rise and take their rightful place in the arena of battle. Young David saw the stalemate. No one challenged Goliath. David couldn't stand it. He offered himself to God. God is looking for someone like that today—someone who can't live with evil, who can't stomach the perversion, and is enraged to see God dishonored. God is looking for someone He can use to turn the tide in America.

There are many more things we can do to get out of fear and get into victory. Here is the great promise: when God sees someone take up the mighty weapons of the Spirit, in the Name of Jesus, and attempt the impossible, He will muster all the resources of heaven to bring that someone total victory.

Now let me tell you what I know God is saying to you: do not wait for things to get better. Do not wait for the lukewarm leaders to wake up. Do not look for a special sign. You have permission—whether or not anyone else agrees with you—to save America.

I am only going to make two points.

1. Do not doubt that you and God are more than enough to win this war.

2. It is because God is with you that you are going to be triumphant!

*Then Jonathan said to the young man who bore his armor, "Come, let us go over to the garrison of these uncircumcised; it may be that the Lord will work for us. For nothing restrains the Lord from saving by many or by few"* (1 Samuel 14:6).

Child of God, you are more than enough to turn the tide. Your burden for America is your best weapon. Forget all about exotic prophecies and emotional experiences. The pilot light to your great adventure is in your burden for your nation. That burden is there for a reason.

When evil is exalted, God looks for deliverers. He scans the nation to see who will separate themselves from the carnal Church and the intoxicated preachers. He looks for those who will allow God to make them the indestructible voices who will restore righteousness to America.

"Now thanks be unto God who always causes us to triumph in Christ!" He does not awaken us to action just to frustrate us. He jolts us awake in order to ignite a string of miracles and reveal His plan.

"Come, let us go!" is the watchword of this hour.

Our tent crusades in California were not condoned by state law. But I obeyed the real law and the higher law. Gavin Newsom, the governor of California, not only violated the law of the land, which is the Constitution, but also violated the highest law—which was God's voice, telling me to go. That is why our meetings exploded with decisions for Christ and miracles.

And you also have permission to go!

> Then the Spirit of the Lord will come upon you, and you will prophesy with them and be turned into another man. And let it be, when these signs come to you, that you do as the occasion demands; for God is with you (1 Samuel 10:6-7).

Do as the occasion demands. The tepid teachers who refuse to obey God are saying things that sound right, but they are completely wrong for the occasion. This is no time for apologies, camouflage, or passivity. The occasion demands action. But not just any action. It demands a Holy Ghost-filled vessel to do anything and everything that is now justified by the occasion.

Some will read this and say there is not enough information. Those are the chilly souls you need to get away from. Those are the people who are not looking for guidance, they are just seeking an excuse. The people this message is targeting have already heard from God. They are ready to launch. They just needed permission.

What are you waiting for? God has given you permission! Now, let's go save America!

# Chapter 12

# A Massive Number of Christians Are Experiencing a Strange Miracle

And we are discovering that this was predicted—in detail.

The Holy Spirit is separating them. He has selected them for special grace and power to accomplish mighty acts at the edge of history. They will be uniquely equipped to face the sophisticated evil of our time. But it all begins by making peace with the Holy Spirit and restoring His rightful place in our hearts and in the Church.

Take a close look at the Book of Acts and you will see the disarming, down-to-earth way that first-century believers related to the Holy Spirit. While they revered Him deeply, they had a sense of His nearness and His involvement in their day-to-day operations.

They behaved as if He was so near that they could almost see Him. Most of all, they anticipated His instructions.

> *As they ministered to the Lord and fasted, the Holy Spirit said, "Now separate to Me Barnabas and Saul for the work to which I have called them." Then, having fasted and prayed, and laid hands on them, they sent them away. So, being sent out by the Holy Spirit, they went down to Seleucia, and from there they sailed to Cyprus* (Acts 13:2-4).

Millions are now hearing the same call: *"Separate unto Me!"* The Holy Spirit told David Wilkerson about this coming separation and how pockets of prophetic people would huddle together across our nation. He said:

> God-hungry people are saying among themselves, "This is not it. There is something more. The bigness and the sensationalism of it all has left us empty and dry. We want more. More than entertainment. More than big, showy buildings. More than a shallow celebrity gospel. We want deeper values. We want to see Jesus. We want spotless robes of righteousness. We want to go back to doing things in total dependence on God."[1]

Many of these people were chased out of churches that were once fiery, Spirit-filled churches that had taken on a new "seeker-friendly" format. They saw their church now focused on church growth, downplaying the presence of the Holy Spirit, and programs designed for the sole purpose of attracting outsiders. They felt punished for wanting a move of God.

They are fed up with the world system—especially when they see it operating in the Church.

They can't stomach the glitzy entertainment centers anymore. They believe we have no time to play games. They are frustrated that the Church is catering to the lukewarm members.

They are done with egocentric preachers with grandiose, expensive, and carnal visions that have nothing to do with soul-winning or revival. They accuse these preachers of being distracted—even derailed from their first love. Disciples are abandoning "attraction" churches, and in their hearts something revolutionary is happening. God is starting a fresh movement.

David Wilkerson explained more of what he saw coming: "God is revealing to all praying people that a glorious new work of the Spirit is about to break forth. God is going to shake everything that can be shaken. He will tear down the old political, backslidden, ecclesiastical system. He will disown the formal, super-church structure. He will chase out of His presence all who are engaging in self-promoting ministries."[2]

The praying people he mentions will force changes. They are a new breed for a new need. They are frustrated, hungry, and their numbers are growing fast. They are coalescing around certain truths—fasting, repentance, and holy surrender to Christ.

Smith Wigglesworth saw this separation coming, way back in 1927. He predicted the same group of people that David Wilkerson described, "All the people which are pressing into and getting ready for this glorious attained place where they shall not be found naked, where they shall be blameless, where they shall be immovable, where they shall be purified by the power of the Word of God, have within them a consciousness of the very presence of

God within, changing their very nature and preparing them for a greater thing, and causing them to be ready for translation."[3]

Both men believed that this gathering unto the Holy Spirit would begin after a great falling away.

Wigglesworth said, "We have to see that these days have to come, before the Lord can come. There has to be a falling away. ...There are in the world two classes of believers. There are believers which are disobedient, or I ought to say there are children which are saved by the power of God which are disobedient children. And there are children which are just the same saved by the power of God, who all the time are longing to be more obedient."[4]

I know that the moment predicted by these two men is upon us. Every day, I receive another account of frustrated saints who have been suddenly driven to hours of prayer. Many are fasting.

A vast number are about to find each other in a true outbreak of holy fire. Millions of believers across America feel they are being separated to the Holy Spirit for some amazing yet unknown reason. David Wilkerson talked about a "work" within us. Smith Wigglesworth talked about "pressing in." The image is clear. The Holy Spirit is stirring souls across the nation. They are done with the overuse of big screens, skinny jeans, and fog machines.

The weapons of our warfare are not carnal, but mighty through God to the pulling down of strongholds!

These frustrated saints are being pulled away from fleshly things, even as a spirit of prayer is overtaking them. They are surrendering to a special work of the Holy Spirit. A fresh work of the Holy Spirit has begun, and the impact will soon be widespread in all the earth!

## Notes

1. David Wilkerson, "End-Time Values," World Challenge, https://www.worldchallenge.org/end-time-values.
2. Ibid.
3. Smith Wigglesworth, "Preparation for the Second Coming of the Lord, Part 1," Angelus Temple, Bible Study #21, August 11, 1927, http://www.smithwigglesworth.com/index.php/smith-wigglesworth-sermons/miscellaneous-sermons/preparation-for-the-second-coming-1.
4. Ibid.

# Chapter 13

# WE ARE STANDING AT THE RED SEA

THINGS LOOK IMPOSSIBLE, BUT THAT IS A GOOD THING.

While millions were watching on their TVs and devices, the host of the show asked me, "What moment are we at in this country?" I answered, "The American Church is at the Red Sea."

Much of the American Church believes this is a time of fear, despair, and profound disappointment. It is a time of dreadful uncertainty. It seems that the promises given to us by preachers have popped like so many balloons. Many regret having stood with Trump. Others are abandoning their convictions in order to please a fallen culture. Still others are stunned and confused by the bizarre events unfolding every day.

*Divisions spread like earthquake faults.* Many are pointing fingers. It would seem that we need someone to arise and bring us a soothing balm. Someone to console us. *But the fact is, we need a swift kick.*

The Israelites were backed up against an impenetrable sea. A vast army, blind with revenge, was bearing down on them. Were they right to fear and be dismayed? Were they right to rail against Moses and remind him that they never wanted this adventure? "Is this not the word that we told you in Egypt, saying, 'Let us alone that we may serve the Egyptians'? For it would have been better for us to serve the Egyptians than that we should die in the wilderness" (Exod. 14:12).

*Isn't this what we are hearing right now?* Some are saying, "It's better for us to serve wokeness than to hold on to this embarrassing hope." Moses tried to rally the people.

> *And Moses said to the people, "Do not be afraid. Stand still, and see the salvation of the Lord, which He will accomplish for you today. For the Egyptians whom you see today, you shall see again no more forever. The Lord will fight for you, and you shall hold your peace"* (Exodus 14:13-14).

But remember this—God found fault with Moses' behavior. It was not a time to console, but to command. "And the Lord said to Moses, 'Why do you cry to Me? Tell the children of Israel to go forward'" (Exod. 14:15).

Why did God take a harsh tone with Moses? It was because their fear made no sense and because their statement that slavery was better was blasphemy.

These people had witnessed nine astounding miracles in Egypt. *The simple progression of God's acts should have been more than enough proof that another miracle was inevitable.*

Do you mean to tell me you have forgotten the progression of miracles that have brought us to this point? "Cyrus" came to the White House. The collusion attack failed. The Obama-led FBI failed to run Trump out of office. The economy boomed, despite the attempts of every Democrat, every media outlet, and Big Tech undermining him. Victory upon victory led us to a golden age for the middle class and the Church. And what? God has abandoned us now? Why would that be?

Now we are at the Red Sea. And just as the Israelites should have expected a miracle, so should we.

The uncovering of the vast corruption, evil, and manipulation perpetrated by Biden and the Democrat-controlled states would never have happened unless God was behind it. The Lord revealed a threat to our freedom that was lodged in our foundation like a time bomb.

*Wake up, Church! This is a test!* The images of dread and fear are a test. The feeling that immorality will swallow our nation whole is a test. The draining depression brought on by the election is a test.

Think back to the time when King Jehoshaphat turned a hopeless situation into proof that a miracle was coming. Read carefully what he said:

> *And now, here are the people of Ammon, Moab, and Mount Seir—whom You would not let Israel invade when they came out of the land of Egypt, but they turned from them and did not destroy them—here they are, rewarding us by coming to throw us out of Your possession which You have given us to inherit. O our God, will You not judge them? For we have*

> *no power against this great multitude that is coming*
> *against us; nor do we know what to do, but our eyes*
> *are upon You* (2 Chronicles 20:10-12).

Let's look at the lessons in these words for us right now. Jehoshaphat reminded God, "A great army is coming to take away something You gave us." Then the king reminded the enemy, "How is that going to work? Do you really want to mess with land that God gave to us Jews?"

*In the same way, America is a miracle.* We did not come about by our own wits or our own greatness. Do you believe that voting machines from Venezuela or China are going to dislodge the home of the brave and the land of the free, without God stepping in?

Next, the king said to Jehovah, "Will You not judge them?" Great evil will not go unpunished. Of course not!

Finally, Jehoshaphat said to God, "We have no wisdom for this and we have no might against them, but we are looking to You." Similarly, this is also a test! God wants the glory. God will bring this wickedness down by His own hand.

*We found out that too many American Christians are flat-out wimps.* Wimpy worship, wimpy convictions, wimpy prayers, and wimpy loyalty to God. But the remnant found out something exactly the opposite.

Their hope is in God—and nothing else. They are ready to obey their marching orders. Preachers should not be cowards and traitors. They need to tell the people to move forward. We should be outraged that our election was stolen and our votes were nullified! Don't you get it? We are not Venezuela—we are America!

We should be moving forward. We should not be debating how much we can do—we should be doing all we can. Get rid of that lie that we should appear polite and compliant in the face of this vile coup. We need to file every lawsuit necessary to expose every villain involved in this crime—even if they are Republicans.

It is not wrong to reject this fraudulent administration. It is not wrong to exhaust every legal option. It is not wrong to make all the noise we need to make in order to take down this monster. God wants to open the Red Sea before us. He just wants us to stop feeling sorry for ourselves and move forward into our miracle!

# Chapter 14

# IT'S TIME FOR THE EAGLES TO LEAVE THE TURKEY YARD

*When the eagles are silent, the parrots begin to jabber.*
—WINSTON CHURCHILL

IT IS CLEAR, AS THE MADNESS SPREADS AND THE CHURCH just wrings its hands, that it is time for the eagles to leave the turkey yard. You know who you are, you who are an eagle. There's a fire inside you that you can't put out. You are ruined for "Church-As-Usual-Incorporated." For too long you've been told to be a good little birdie. "Don't ruffle any feathers!" But you just can't stomach the stale kernels they toss to you any longer. You must have fresh meat.

All around you, the turkeys peck at the ground. But all you can see are the clouds and the sky, where you know you belong. You long to be home, where the glory is. Your place is alongside the heroes of faith who changed the course of nations. "Survival-mode teaching" sickens you. The idea that tepid happiness is the goal enrages you.

You made the mistake of looking at old YouTube videos. You saw Oral Roberts. You saw Kathryn Kuhlman. You saw Smith Wigglesworth. You jumped up and screamed, "But where are the miracles *today?*" You made the mistake of listening to old preaching tapes, where you heard men and women preaching holy fire! They didn't do monologues. They didn't do stand-up comedy. They pulled the pin out of Bible verses and flung them like grenades to explode into the souls of their audience.

You heard people sobbing at the altars. You heard them linger until something real and lasting transformed them. Then something really painful happened to you—you looked at your generation. You saw the national cancer of wickedness. You saw the insane brainwashing. You saw the limp-wristed tactics of the lukewarm Church.

You became like David as he stared at the paralyzed army of Israel cowering before a defiant Goliath. You cried, *"Why doesn't somebody do something?"* So now that you realize that *the "somebody" is you*, it is too late for you. The die is cast. You've gone too far to turn back. You now know too much. You feel like you should leave before you hurt someone. You remember the verse, "They that wait upon the Lord shall renew their strength; they shall mount up with wings as eagles" (Isa. 40:31 KJV).

*Prayer is your escape from the prison yard of compromise and mediocrity.* We're not talking about the "gobble-gobble prayers" you heard in the yard—we're talking about *falling before God and waiting upon Him until you come forth as pure gold.*

What are we talking about? We are talking about prayer that heaven can't resist and hell can't stand. The kind of prayer that breaks the grip of ancient demonic strongholds. Prayer that causes students to begin to weep on campus, even though they do not know why. Prayer that fills people with the Holy Spirit. Prayer that removes fear and instills unshakable courage to tell a generation the genuine Good News, the mighty Gospel—which is the unapologetic, undeniable, unstoppable power of God!

*Eagles dare, while turkeys stare!* Eagles are born out of prayer. They spring forth from the hand of God, fully convinced of their destiny and their goal. Let mistaken millennials protest against the AR-15. You take hold of John 17:15, "My prayer is not that you take them out of the world but that you protect them from the evil one" (NIV). That is your battle cry! You don't want out. You know the Lord Jesus will keep you from the evil one! You are ready to soar into any nest of evil and destroy the works of the devil. Where eagles gather, power is present.

*Where eagles gather, the deep purposes of Almighty God are revealed.* Where eagles gather, there's no self-pity, no encounter sessions, and no hiding in your "safe space." When turkeys are transformed into eagles, they are equipped, they are ignited, and they are fitted for war. Eagles must have a challenge. They yearn for a cause that will summon up all of their strength, talent, and time. They want something they can easily imagine doing for the rest of their lives.

*It's time for you to fly out of the turkey yard and never look back!*

# Chapter 15

# A New Kind of Christian Will Soon Appear in America

REMEMBER WHEN I TOLD YOU THIS: A NEW KIND OF Christian leader will soon appear on the American stage. They will not fit any present mold. They will be the catalysts. They will usher in the next great awakening. They will appear because conditions will demand their appearance. Consider how the coronavirus could be the pretext to change the very way churches and ministries operate. Even to the point of banning public gatherings. In the next few years, you will likely see social media virtually remove all preaching. Not only that, but there will be a concerted effort to marginalize the Church in ways you never imagined. So does that mean that Bible-based Christianity is over in America? Absolutely not!

You watch: God will come out of nowhere to meet this threat. A big difference you will see in the coming leaders is where they serve. A few of them will be in pulpits. More of them will be in politics, business, science, law, entertainment, music, or a thousand other fields of endeavor.

They will not introduce subjects—they will introduce eras.

No one will be able to buy them off or get them to change the subject. They will operate on a disquieting plane of holiness and consecration. I believe A.W. Tozer was describing them when he said, "They serve God and mankind from motives too high to be understood by the rank and file of religious retainers who, today, shuttle in and out of the sanctuary."

Today they suffer. Their agony is what happens when worlds collide. They see their destiny. It's big and dangerous. A part of them glories in the potential to know God intimately and represent Him bravely. They see themselves rebuking kings, tyrants, and warmongers. They see themselves commanding the transfer of the wealth of the wicked into the control of the righteous (see Isa. 60:5).

God is warring to save America. You must find your assignment in that war. But how can we know our assignment? The secret to finding your assignment is your heart. God speaks to the heart and then the heart must control the mind.

Today, many Spirit-filled believers are unwittingly involved in New Age practices. They relate to God as if He were some kind of "force" rather than a Person. They think that audacity and confidence will unlock gifts, authority, and direction. They speak of "activating gifts" as if there was a formula to supernatural manifestations. My friend, it comes through brokenness, not arrogance. The "force" is a farce.

The gifts and anointing of the Holy Spirit always come through relationship. Sorry, but Christianity has always been and always will be family owned and operated. So then, how can we know our assignment?

Your assignment in the Army of God is your individual expression and extension of Christ's destruction of the works of the devil. You are a destroyer of the works of the devil.

> *For this purpose the Son of God was manifested, that He might destroy the works of the devil* (1 John 3:8).

God will give you a way to do it that is unique to you. Until that gets through to you—until you admit and agree to those terms—God will remain silent about your assignment. Because the situation today in America is an impossible one, only one kind of person will make a difference now. They must be armed with divine certainty. They must own an unshakable, bone-deep conviction that they have been chosen for this task. Without this, we have zero hope of removing the bloody talons of satan from the throat of our nation. Without it, we are doomed to another embarrassing misfire, pawned off as revival.

Next, you must face the fact that very few believers are supposed to be teachers, preachers, or pastors (see James 3:1). For too long, we have listened to the voice of God through a filter. In the past, whenever God has moved someone to serve Him, we have assumed it meant "ministry."

This assumption of ministry has sent many Christians to Bible college who didn't belong there.

Worse yet, it has filled pulpits with people who should have never been ordained. This reminds me of why President Woodrow Wilson once said, "One of the proofs of the divinity of the Gospel is the preaching it has survived."

This filtered view of service is one big reason the Church lost influence in our nation. God tried to send people into education, law, medicine, business, art, media, and yes, even politics—but instead, we herded them into "Christian service." You see it in the Bible. You see it in the stories of heroes of faith throughout history who altered the course of their generation. At the dawn of their mission, God infused them with incontestable certainty. This certainty plays a critical role in their survival.

Think of it like the escape velocity of a rocket. Escape velocity is one of the biggest challenges of space travel. In order for a rocket to break free of the Earth's gravitational force it must reach a speed of seven miles per second. That's 25,000 miles per hour!

Evil convulses at the approach of a new vessel of God. Hell instantly puts those who are chosen on a hit list. The child of God must be blasted by divine certainty into a trajectory that will escape the pull of devils, the seduction of fame, withering criticism, and that "dark night of the soul" that comes to all who are called of God.

From his death bed, John Wesley wrote his last letter to William Wilberforce to encourage him as he fought in England's Parliament to abolish slavery. In this letter, Wesley confirms the urgency of divine certainty, "Unless God has raised you up for this very thing, you will be worn out by the opposition of men and devils. But if God be for you, who can be against you? Are all of them together stronger than God? O be not weary of well doing! Go on, in the name of God and in the power of his might."

Understand this, child of God! The same Spirit that is awakening a passion and direction in you is doing the same thing to millions more. Soon an army will emerge that will invade every area of our culture. Today it is sporadic fire, here and there, but soon the prophetic core of God will obey and embrace their assignment. They will come together in a chorus of victory that will be unlike anything we have ever seen.

Never forget—Christianity will survive without America, but *America will not survive without Christianity.*

# Chapter 16

# GO AFTER GOD
# AND MAKE
# SOMETHING HAPPEN

NEVER HAVE I BEEN MORE SOLEMN ABOUT ANYTHING I HAVE ever written. Never have I felt the need to risk whatever credibility I may have with you. I am going against the grain of making predictions.

Many predictors are driven by the desperate need to console the weary American Church. They are talking the way they did before the pandemic and before the Biden debacle. They are telling you that we are about to be relieved and no longer on a war-footing. They are saying that we can now return to a peacetime church culture.

Not only are they horribly wrong, their message will leave you open to the attack of the enemy. Their words may be sweet to the taste but, in the end, they will be bitter in your stomach (see Rev.

10:9). Do not let them distract you or keep you from contending for a national miracle. Do not go chasing after predictions.

*We as American Christians and patriots must become a united army in a desperate battle.* The most important thing to impress upon an army is the reality of the threat. There is no way around it.

Army of God! *You must have it drilled into you that we are facing a long and hard road ahead.*

We as the American Church no longer need to have our ego stroked. We need someone to raise our morale as we prepare for war.

Winston Churchill faced this very task. On May 10, 1940, Germany invaded France and the Netherlands. That same day in England, Prime Minister Neville Chamberlain stepped down from his post, and King George VI tapped Winston Churchill to replace him.

World War II was on, and Britain needed the right leader to guide the nation into the gathering storm that had begun to rage across Europe. Unlike Chamberlain and Lord Halifax, politicians who sought peace treaties and truces with Germany, Churchill recognized the necessity of war.

Peace, he thought, meant submission—and submission meant death. On May 13, Churchill gathered his war cabinet and went to address Parliament. The speech he delivered that afternoon, "Blood, Toil, Tears, and Sweat," has become known as one of the most rousing speeches in British history. Churchill's message was simple but powerful—Britain must fight, and Britain must win.

Churchill said these immortal words:

> I would say to the House, as I said to those who have joined this government, "I have nothing to offer but blood, toil, tears, and sweat."

We have before us an ordeal of the most grievous kind. We have before us many, many long months of struggle and of suffering. You ask, what is our policy? I can say: It is to wage war, by sea, land and air, with all our might and with all the strength that God can give us; to wage war against a monstrous tyranny, never surpassed in the dark, lamentable catalogue of human crime. That is our policy.

You ask, what is our aim? I can answer in one word: It is victory, victory at all costs, victory in spite of all terror, victory, however long and hard the road may be, for without victory, there is no survival.[1]

China, Facebook, Twitter, YouTube, CNN, Hollywood, and the Democrat Party have woven the most insidious and vile web of deceit in American history. For all real Americans, it is our version of "a monstrous tyranny never surpassed in the dark, lamentable catalogue of human crime."

Thousands of pulpits, at this hour, believe the message of consolation is the message of the hour. No! It is not! *We do not need comfort. We need outrage. We need the white-hot rage of a people who will not go gentle into that dark night.* Do not hesitate or surrender. Instead of watching things happen—*make something happen.*

Our final answer to them is, "No! We do not accept the bitter bread of surrender and capitulation! No! You will not educate our children by wading them into a godless swamp. No! You will not steal our small businesses and our churches. No! You will not offer us as a living sacrifice to Communist China. We will not bow. We will not surrender. Not ever!"

*This is not a time for soothing lambs but for igniting lions.* It is time to say to satan, "We have not even begun to fight." Beyond January 6—beyond January 20—beyond whatever human deadline has been declared. We are not going to stop. We are not going to slow down. Our ranks are closing. Our numbers are growing. Our fortitude and resolve are intensifying.

Our struggle for America is not ending—it is just beginning. The enemy needs to know we are never going away.

Again, to quote Churchill, "This is the lesson: never give in, never give in, never, never, never, never, in nothing, great or small, large or petty...Never yield to force; never yield to the apparently overwhelming might of the enemy."

I know I have been given this mandate: Forget predictions about what will happen. Instead, go after God and *make* something happen!

## NOTE

1. Winston Churchill, "Blood, Toil, Tears, and Sweat," May 13, 1940, https://winstonchurchill.org/resources/speeches/1940 -the-finest-hour/blood-toil-tears-sweat.

# Chapter 17

# THE EDUCATED BULLET

*Untutored courage is useless in the face of educated bullets.*
—GENERAL GEORGE S. PATTON

PATTON SAID, "UNTUTORED COURAGE IS USELESS IN THE face of educated bullets." He said that in 1922, but his words are perfect for today—especially for the American Church.

A soldier who has bravado but no training is easy pickings for a trained enemy. It is equally true that a zealous believer without training is easy prey for the devil. How can a church that is just barely keeping its head above water ever find training to impact a depraved culture? It is sad but true—the Church is absorbing more darkness from the world than she is giving off light to the world.

Our lack of power and influence has shrunk to disastrous levels. If the trend continues much longer, America is lost forever.

What is maddening is that we are losing this war for all the wrong reasons.

We have the best message, the best book, and the greatest power. But that is not how we look. At best, Christianity is dismissed as a quaint relic and, at worst, as a virus that must be eradicated.

How did this happen? What comes from our pulpits is the culprit. Modern preaching is persistently therapeutic. Such preaching inevitably makes emotional recovery the priority. Ask yourself: How did self-help become the goal in a movement based on self-denial? That is a tribute to the devil's power to deceive.

So, how can we reverse this disaster? The answer is by two important steps.

*First, we must admit we are in a war.* We must understand warfare. We are losing because we do not believe we are in a war. Therapeutic Christianity cannot fathom war. It finds it repugnant.

Those who deny the existence of a war between good and evil have also rejected the Bible. If there is anything clear and consistent in the Word of God, it is war. The New Testament is full of references to weapons, armor, tactics, and many other military terms.

*Second, we must become educated bullets.* America does not need believers who must always "feel good." America needs Christians who are educated bullets. To get there, we need training. Training, above all, is essential if we are to win any war.

Peter exhorts us: "But sanctify the Lord God in your hearts, and always be ready to give a defense to everyone who asks you a reason for the hope that is in you, with meekness and fear" (1 Pet. 3:15).

Training was a priority to Christ!

> *Go therefore and make disciples of all the nations,*
> *baptizing them in the name of the Father and of the*
> *Son and of the Holy Spirit, teaching them to observe*
> *all things that I have commanded you; and lo, I am*
> *with you always, even to the end of the age* (Matthew
> 28:19-20).

We are making a lot of things, but not many disciples. The early Church did not have a feel-good message. Neither did it produce feel-good believers.

Too many American Christians do not know what they believe or why they believe it. They cannot withstand the corruption of our sick society. Their endless quest to hold on to "groovy feelings" guarantees we will never save our nation from destruction.

When the Holy Spirit was poured out on the day of Pentecost, the early Church could have easily turned that blessing into an excuse for gorging on emotion. They could have formed a secret society that endlessly soaked in the presence of God. Instead, the Holy Spirit immediately drove them out of the relative safety of the upper room and out to the masses gathered in Jerusalem.

But they stopped there.

And then, after thousands were saved, they could have retreated into festive fellowship. But the disciples knew better. So did the new converts. Training was the order of the day.

> *And they continued steadfastly in the apostles' doctrine*
> [teaching] *and fellowship, in the breaking of bread,*
> *and in prayers. Then fear came upon every soul, and*

*many wonders and signs were done through the apostles* (Acts 2:42-43).

The apostles understood that the Church must be saturated with the Word of God. They saw the urgency of right doctrine and fervent prayer. Look at modern Church growth models. In virtually every model, doctrine and prayer are the first things to go. And it goes further than that—there is an anti-Bible spirit in many churches. Even in Spirit-filled churches.

The doctrines that the disciples taught were the very words of Jesus. Words remembered and quickened by the Holy Spirit were arranged into our New Testament. Those words were so orderly, in fact, that they are called the Apostle's Doctrine. Remember again what Jesus said: "Teaching them to observe all things that I have commanded you" (Matt. 28:20). Early disciples were trained on the words of Jesus!

The early Church did not depend on ethereal emotions or inner impressions. They relied on the work of the Holy Spirit who is unswervingly committed to the Word of God. If you turn your back on the Bible, the Holy Spirit will stop speaking to you.

*Do you want to be trained?* Do you want to be an educated bullet? Do you want the training so that you can make a glorious noise before you leave this earth? Here's how to get the training.

Our training begins with these verses:

*I beseech you therefore, brethren, by the mercies of God, that you present your bodies a living sacrifice, holy, acceptable to God, which is your reasonable service. And do not be conformed to this world, but be transformed by the renewing of your mind, that you may prove what is that good and acceptable and perfect will of God* (Romans 12:1-2).

1.  Training for spiritual warfare begins by emptying yourself of false teaching. Some incorrect teaching has been put into your spirit. Those false ideas will strive against your training. To embrace true training, you must recognize and reject any false training you received in the past.

2.  You must surrender your right to a personal opinion. You are a soldier, not a consultant. You have *orders* from King Jesus, not talking points. War is too urgent for double-mindedness or hesitation in following orders.

3.  You must maintain this training attitude for the remainder of your life. You are not testing the waters. You are not coming into this to see how it goes. This is a discipline you will walk in for the rest of your life.

4.  You must find your assignment. There is something you are supposed to do before you leave. There is something you are supposed to shout from the rooftops.

In the earlier chapters we saw the monster. Then we saw what was at stake. After that we saw what we must do—no matter what it takes. Finally, we saw Paul model what it means to not leave quietly. And now, we start our training. You should see the rest of this book as a training manual. A training manual for you to find and use your voice.

*The greatest weapon God has given you is a voice.* Your voice is not supposed to be silent. It is not supposed to be silenced. Never underestimate the power of a voice. With just their voice, heroes of God have defeated armies and raised the dead. The world was created by the Voice of God.

Many verses tell us about the power of our God-given voice. Isaiah wrote, "And He has made My mouth like a sharp sword" (Isa. 49:2).

> *The Lord God has given Me the tongue of the learned* [trained], *that I should know how to speak a word in season to him who is weary. He awakens Me morning by morning; He awakens My ear to hear as the learned* (Isaiah 50:4).

But the greatest promise refers to our time and this present darkness. Jesus said, "For I will give you a mouth and wisdom which all your adversaries will not be able to contradict or resist" (Luke 21:15).

The training God will give you will not only remove fear, it will make you bold as a lion to face the enemy. Louis Wilson said, "The aim of military training is not just to prepare men for battle, but to make them long for it."

That convulsion you felt in the background is satan. He just felt pain because you said that you were going to start your training. You have decided to be a living weapon that is honed, crafted, and empowered to speak up, speak out, and devastate evil with a tongue of fire!

Section Three

FIREPOWER

# Chapter 18

# FIREPOWER: HOW EVERYDAY PEOPLE DESTROY EVIL

HOW DO EVERYDAY PEOPLE DESTROY EVIL? THE ANSWER IS *firepower*. Firepower is a word that has come to mean a lot more to me during these dark days. To appreciate firepower, we must go way beyond its military definition:

## FIREPOWER

a. The number of weapons and ammunition in your arsenal.

b. The amount of destruction those weapons and ammunition can inflict on the enemy.

c. The skill level of your army to implement weapons and ammunition.

Now let's take that definition a step further. To the Army of God, it means even more.

The best verse I can think of to define our firepower is:

> *For the weapons of our warfare are not physical [weapons of flesh and blood], but they are mighty before God for the overthrow and destruction of strongholds, [inasmuch as we] refute arguments and theories and reasonings and every proud and lofty thing that sets itself up against the [true] knowledge of God; and we lead every thought and purpose away captive into the obedience of Christ (the Messiah, the Anointed One)* (2 Corinthians 10:4-5 AMPC).

Firepower is clearly seen in these verses. First, in the might of the weapons themselves—they overthrow and destroy. Second, their might is through God. That means unlimited power and supply. Third, it says, "we lead every thought and purpose away captive into the obedience of Christ." That speaks of an astonishing skill level.

So something must be desperately missing because American Christianity is constantly losing ground to the enemy. You have felt it in church. We are just not doing enough damage to the works of the devil.

This section of the book is about the missing pieces of effectiveness—the missing parts that blunt our ability to drive back evil.

How do we get from here to *firepower?* By being brutally honest. It is amazing how often the first step to any victory starts with coming clean about your current condition.

You must make lifelong decisions and permanent changes. You must ask yourself, "What is it I will never do again?" And, "What is it that I will never stop doing?"

Let's review our journey so far. I hope you have changed your mind about some things since you started reading this book. Let's review them.

The right course of action is only possible with a high level of urgency. We must know what is truly at stake. The agenda of the Democrat Party must be stopped.

Their voting act will codify the fraud of the last election and guarantee that there will never again be any free and fair elections.

Critical Race Theory: Democrats are leading the charge to teach our children to hate America through the racist teachings of Critical Race Theory.

Their Equality Act will put males in the girls' bathroom in grammar schools and in churches. It will also make it a hate crime to preach biblical Christianity.

Their vaccination passports are an early version of the Mark of the Beast that will be needed to buy, sell, travel, and make a living. Biden has stated, "The rule is simple. Get vaccinated or wear a mask before you do."

*And, once and for all, let's kill the excuse of "not getting political."* We did not start this fight. We did not "become political." *They* became spiritual. They jumped into *our* yard.

From the Book of Esther we learned that doing your duty is not as dangerous as not doing your duty.

> *And Mordecai told them to answer Esther: "Do not think in your heart that you will escape in the king's*

DO NOT LEAVE QUIETLY

*palace any more than all the other Jews. For if you remain completely silent at this time, relief and deliverance will arise for the Jews from another place, but you and your father's house will perish. Yet who knows whether you have come to the kingdom for such a time as this?"*

*Then Esther told them to reply to Mordecai: "Go, gather all the Jews who are present in Shushan, and fast for me; neither eat nor drink for three days, night or day. My maids and I will fast likewise. And so I will go to the king, which is against the law; and if I perish, I perish!"* (Esther 4:13-16)

*We now understand Romans 13 and Christian civil disobedience.* Some say, "But I was told that Romans 13 tells Christians not to speak out against rulers—isn't that right? Doesn't verse 2 of Romans 13 say, 'Therefore whoever resists the authority resists the ordinance of God, and those who resist will bring judgment on themselves'?" Let's read Romans 13:1-4 one more time:

*Let every soul be subject to the governing authorities. For there is no authority except from God, and the authorities that exist are appointed by God. Therefore whoever resists the authority resists the ordinance of God, and those who resist will bring judgment on themselves. For rulers are not a terror to good works, but to evil. Do you want to be unafraid of the authority? Do what is good, and you will have praise from the same. For he is God's minister to you for good. But if you do evil, be afraid; for he does not bear the sword in vain; for he is God's minister, an avenger to execute wrath on him who practices evil.*

*You can now see that those authorities who are of God are* not *a terror to good works.* Any government that terrorizes the innocent is not of God. Do you think that Hitler was God's will for Germany? Hitler and other tyrants are in fact the ones being warned that there were God-appointed governments who would destroy them, "But if you do evil, be afraid; for he does not bear the sword in vain; for he is God's minister, an avenger to execute wrath on him who practices evil." That is why the just powers of the world rose up and destroyed the Nazis.

*They praise good works.* Authorities that are endorsed by God do not hate or oppose Christian activity. They are the ones who—even if they are not Christian themselves—do not insult soul-winning or fight the work of God. They are the law enforcement officers, the teachers, and the politicians who are glad that children are getting out of gangs and off of drugs.

*Now let's see it in action, in your life, with this question:* "What would you do if they expelled your young daughter from school for being a Christian?" What if it had nothing to do with bad behavior? She was expelled for her beliefs, pure and simple. What would you do? You would storm down to the principal's office and demand your rights as a parent and a citizen.

You could also understand your fellow believer doing the same thing if this happened to one of their children. One thing you would not do is accuse your neighbor of being judgmental, political, or "not walking in love."

Many Christians think that speaking out against Biden, Schumer, Pelosi, the IRS, or local politicians is "different" than parents protecting their children against coercive schools.

Oh really? How is it different? The only thing I can see that is different is that it hasn't hit home yet. So far, we have seen executives fired for defending traditional marriage, the IRS attacking pastors and parents, healthcare hijacked, and our phone calls monitored. If they do all of this today, what will they do tomorrow?

You say, "If my child were to be banished for being a Christian, I would act!" The problem is that, if you wait till that time, it will be too late. The local school is the final stop for tyranny. Before there can be a blatant attempt to ban Christianity at school, a lot of other bad things must first take place, and they are.

Their plan is that the public must be reprogrammed to accept the loss of freedom. Tyranny trickles down through several layers like acid eating its way down to the hull of a ship.

The ruling authority of the United States is the Constitution, something those in the government have all sworn to uphold and protect. Instead, it has been the unswerving passion of the present administration to undermine the first four amendments to the Constitution, setting aside those guarantees:

1. Congress shall make no law respecting an establishment of religion, or prohibiting the free exercise thereof; or abridging the freedom of speech, or of the press; or the right of the people peaceably to assemble, and to petition the government for a redress of grievances.

2. A well-regulated militia being necessary to the security of a free state, the right of the people to keep and bear arms shall not be infringed.

3. No soldier shall, in time of peace, be quartered in any house without the consent of the owner, nor in time of war, but in a manner to be prescribed by law.

4. The right of the people to be secure in their persons, houses, papers, and effects, against unreasonable searches and seizures shall not be violated, and no warrants shall issue, but upon probable cause, supported by oath or affirmation, and particularly describing the place to be searched, and the persons or things to be seized.

*Just imagine if they strip the Church of these rights, what chaos and persecution would ensue.*

Let this settle the question. Because if we cannot clear our spirits of compromise, God will not give us the firepower to save our nation.

This is not the first time that Christian leaders have had to reach a painful point of opposition that was not popular. In the 20th century Christian heroes opposed tyranny:

- Pastor Richard Wurmbrand stood alone among more than 1,000 leaders to denounce the control of Romanian communism, and was imprisoned.

- Dietrich Bonhoeffer was a German theologian famous for his stand against Adolf Hitler and the Nazi party. His beliefs and convictions ultimately cost him his life in a Nazi concentration camp.

- Corrie Ten Boom violated German law by hiding Jews in her home and was also sent to a concentration camp.

- Watchman Nee was persecuted for his faith and imprisoned by Chairman Mao. He spent the last twenty years of his life in a Communist Chinese prison.

Each one of these heroes had that moment of denial that said, "This can't be happening!" Yet each one came to that point of clarity in their conscience. Each one said, "This is the right thing to do." Each one faced rejection for trying to convince others of impending tyranny.

It is ironic that each is honored today as a hero, but if they were alive today most American Christians would reject them for their open opposition to political leadership.

Again, 2 Corinthians 10:4 says, "For the weapons of *our warfare* are not physical [weapons of flesh and blood], but they are mighty before God for the overthrow and destruction of strongholds" (AMPC).

The most convicting words of that verse are these: "*our warfare.*" There is no hope for you to ever have mighty weapons until you say, "This is *my* war." Only those who admit they are in a war—that they are soldiers—will be considered for the mighty weapons of God.

This is your war. It is your church's war. It is your family's war.

Remember, we do not activate the gifts of power. The Holy Spirit purifies us and imparts them as He wills. And only those with a heart for war will be considered.

# Chapter 19

# A Time to Fight: Keys to Firepower

THERE IS MOURNING IN AMERICA. SHE FIGHTS FOR HER LIFE as she has not fought since the Civil War. Her muscles fail from exertion; her mind grows weary, frantically seeking answers. For a minute, it looked like she would catch a break from the storm. Instead, new clouds have formed, the angriest winds are raging, and rain is falling like a hail of bullets.

Hope deferred has made the American Dream heartsick. Locusts feed on the American way of life. Our leaders apply cures that are worse than the disease. Nothing seems to work against this maelstrom. Talent does no good. We have a cabinet full of talented failures. Genius is not enough; unrewarded genius is now a proverb. Even education has lost its edge. We are overrun with educated derelicts. No—for this monster, we need something completely different.

*The righteous are the key to restoration*. We hold an entire generation's future in our hands. However, the Bible asks this burning question, "If the foundations be destroyed, what can the righteous do?" (Ps. 11:3). We all know that we must do something drastic. We must do something that will work, but what is it?

In order for us to know what to do we must understand what time it is. This is the missing weapon in our arsenal. Speaking of weapons, 1 Chronicles 12 describes the various fighting skills of the tribes of Israel. The most unique weapon is Issachar. Verse 32 describes them as, "men who had understanding of the times, to know what Israel ought to do." That is the gift we need.

*So what time is it?* It is time to look back at the very first Fourth of July for an important reminder. Having exhausted every means of peaceful resolution, our founding fathers told King George III that it was time to fight. Jefferson penned these immortal words, "We hold these truths to be self-evident, that all men are created equal, that they are endowed by their Creator with certain unalienable Rights, that among these are Life, Liberty and the pursuit of Happiness."

The American dream draws its life from these words. But now an invisible tyrant is taking all that away. Many of the puppets of this tyrant do not even know why they rail against prayer, marriage, and the Word of God, even when it makes no sense.

So what time is it? It is time to fight. I know that we think all we need are words of encouragement. I am sure that this feels like a good time for a word of comfort, but I do not believe that such a word is right. Soothing words will not break the stranglehold on your emotions, your loved ones, your finances, your church, or your nation. It is time to fight! We are flabby from flattering words of spiritual entitlement. Smiley-faced sermons may appease our inner child, but they are powerless against the wolf at the door. We need fighting words!

Few things in history are as awesome as the words of a gifted general. He faces certain defeat, yet finds just the right words that will ignite his troops to impossible victory. This is a time for such words.

> ## WE ARE FLABBY FROM FLATTERING WORDS OF SPIRITUAL ENTITLEMENT.

Americans are in virtually the same condition as were the Jews when they were trying to rebuild the walls of Jerusalem. They forgot their God and made covenants with paganism. They were fearful of opposing the surrounding tribes that did not want a restored Israel. Nehemiah is the general we need today, and his words to the sheepish Jews are the words we need so desperately now:

> *Do not be afraid of the enemy; [earnestly] remember the Lord and imprint Him [on your minds], great and terrible, and [take from Him courage to] fight for your brethren, your sons, your daughters, your wives, and your homes* (Nehemiah 4:14 AMPC).

## FIGHT!

Fight the urge to wallow in self-pity, fight the drowsy spirit that lets you sit passively in front of a screen for hours every day. Fight the pull of compromise and shake yourself for war! You have no time to waste! Fight the images of dread that show you bankrupt, destitute, and diseased. Fight for the power to break destructive habits and relationships. Fight for the courage to face the church board and declare your fiery intention to see revival. Fight your schedule and subdue it for the sake of the Kingdom of God.

*Fight* is a five-letter word. Let each letter be emblazoned in your spirit! Here is how you fight:

### Find your secret place.

*You must designate a place to pray*. You must go there every day. Jesus even suggested a closet! David declared, "Early will I seek You." No warm bed could hold David when the tractor beam of prayer hit his spirit. To say you have no time to pray is to raise the white flag of surrender to the devil. Your secret place will tell you what to do and arm you to do it. In the closet you will meet God and then God will go with you into the battles of your life.

Prayer creates time. It multiplies back the time it uses. How much time did bad decisions use up this week? How many bad people are using up your life right now? People whom prayer would have changed or removed. How many hours went into worrying about problems that, if left at the altar, would have left you with more time? There are miracles all around us and they happen every day. You miss them because of your overactive wits and aggressive need to tackle problems. How many dreams have you postponed because you lacked the courage that prayer imparts?

### Intensify your actions.

When you emerge from the closet of prayer, you will emerge a mighty warrior, who is ready to take the next important step, which is intense action. You must intensify your spirit and become a forceful *doer*. You must attack work, chores, and opportunities.

In 2 Kings 13, the prophet gave the king an amazing opportunity to defeat his enemy. He told him to take arrows and beat the ground with them, knowing that God would strike his enemy with the same force and as many times as he struck the ground. The

King had no fire in his belly for war and love-tapped the ground only three times.

Verse 19 says, "And the man of God was angry with him, and said, 'You should have struck five or six times; then you would have struck Syria till you had destroyed it! But now you will strike Syria only three times.'"

Treat each day as the day that you get to take your shot, and you will do it with all of your might.

### Go beyond.

Doctors told Americans to run for exercise, and we ignored them. Then someone said, "Run a marathon," and running became a craze. That is just the way we are. We really do not want to do something until it is impossible. In the battle you are facing, the surprising problem might be that you are too conservative with your vision. You may be missing the voice of God simply because He has much bigger plans for you than you have for yourself. Small plans have no power to excite men's blood, and they probably will not work out anyway. America needs a flood of visionary Christians who will...

### Be full of faith and vision.

The Holy Spirit can reignite the American spirit through everyday people who choose to shake off the rampant pessimism and negative talk and who build great things for the glory of God. "Going beyond" means living outside of the mundane.

I love this quote by Kenneth J. Jackson, "While real trolleys in Newark, Philadelphia, Pittsburgh, and Boston languish for lack of patronage and government support, millions of people flock to Disneyland to ride fake trains that don't go anywhere."

If you choose to "go beyond," you will take other people with you. Nothing chases away doubt and depression like fresh vision!

## Heal the land.

> *Therefore I remind you to stir up the gift of God which is in you through the laying on of my hands* (2 Timothy 1:6).

Do not neglect your supernatural ministry! I hope you realize that whatever you do to make money is just a front for your true occupation, which is to destroy the works of the devil. Nothing has been a greater passion for me than the truth that every believer is an extension of the healing ministry of Jesus. Not only have we seen people healed on the streets while out witnessing, but the overwhelming number of those who were healed were not believers at the time.

Much has been said about being "purpose driven," but little is actually said about the purpose.

First John 3:8 says, "For this purpose the Son of God was manifested, that He might destroy the works of the devil." Find your career, pay your bills, and love your family, but do not ever forget your ministry of destroying the works of evil. Words of knowledge, prophecies, and acts of supernatural deliverance dwell in you, and the Holy Spirit is discipling and teaching you to express them.

There are many theories about how to save our nation. If you consider the fact that we are running out of time and you factor in the truth that our nation's crisis is truly supernatural, then it follows that the cure is supernatural.

### *Take your place.*

So long as you feel like a second-class citizen, no amount of breakthrough will stick. You will always have the nagging thought in the back of your mind that you do not deserve God's blessings and that they are only temporary. God wants to establish you. Think deeply for a moment about what that means. It means that when you fail, you will get back up. It means that no matter what storms come, you are rooted in God and you are designated by *the Lord Himself* to occupy a special place reserved especially for you. Until you are firmly grounded and established, you will never keep your victories.

As our nation faces her greatest darkness, there must be a new breed of believer roaming the land. Believers who know their God and are known by their God. Christians must emerge who have settled the great questions and do not flinch in the face of adversity. "If God be for us, who can be against us?" cannot be a wistful catchphrase but a core belief that is irrevocably embedded in our hearts.

We must not leave quietly. It is time to fight to bring America back to greatness!

# Chapter 20

# THE DEADLIEST SILENCE: WHEN GOD CANNOT HEAR YOU

GOD DOES NOT HEAR EVERYONE'S PRAYERS. GOD SHUTS OUT some prayers. Proverbs 28:9 says, "One who turns away his ear from hearing the law, even his prayer is an abomination." That is strong stuff. But there are two other pertinent verses.

Psalm 66:18 tells us, "If I regard iniquity in my heart, the Lord will not hear."

And Proverbs 21:13 warns, "Whoever shuts his ears to the cry of the poor will also cry himself and not be heard."

The deadliest silence is when God cannot hear you.

Sure, you care about what happens to America. And yes, you want to be used of the Holy Spirit to drive back evil. But you will be heard on earth only after you have been heard in heaven.

Satan does not respect talent, fame, or eloquence. He does not stand down before men with human prowess who come in the name of God. But he instantly flees before the man whose prayers get through to God.

E.M. Bounds said, "The Church is looking for better methods; God is looking for better men. ...The Holy Ghost does not flow through methods, but through men. He does not come upon machinery, but on men. He does not anoint plans, but men—men of prayer."[1]

Because the world is being flooded with evil, it is spilling over into the Church. Social media has created a swampland of so called "apostles" and "prophets" who are powerless to save America. They are court jesters, providing amusement to bored believers.

Yes, there are true prophets and apostles. But the real ones rarely claim titles. The false ones are constantly claiming things.

They claim to possess gifts of power, but they never do any damage to evil. They are making it all up. They influence gullible believers to chase "words" from God. They create prophetic junkies seeking a daily fix. Meanwhile, their Bibles gather dust.

Many are ignorant of what satan is doing to the nation. Worse still, they are totally ignorant of the role God wants them to play in rescuing our nation.

We have never seen so many fakes in the ministry doing so much harm to the Church. But we should not be surprised. Paul told us that in the last days, they would come in bigger numbers. "But evil men and impostors will grow worse and worse, deceiving and being deceived" (2 Tim. 3:13).

God considers them His enemy. They are a destructive force in the Church, and they are heaping disaster on both those who listen to them and upon themselves. Matthew Henry wrote this about 2 Timothy 3:13:

[Paul] warns Timothy of the fatal end of seducers, as a reason why he should stick closely to the truth as it is in Jesus: But evil men and seducers shall wax worse and worse, etc., v. 13. Observe, as good men, by the grace of God, grow better and better, so bad men, through the subtlety of Satan and the power of their own corruptions, grow worse and worse. The way of sin is down-hill; for such proceed from bad to worse, deceiving and being deceived. Those who deceive others do but deceive themselves; those who draw others into error run themselves into more and more mistakes, and they will find it so at last, to their cost.[2]

Next, Paul warns Timothy that in the last days we must constantly press into the safety of prayer and reading the Word of God.

> *But you must continue in the things which you have learned and been assured of, knowing from whom you have learned them, and that from childhood you have known the Holy Scriptures, which are able to make you wise for salvation through faith which is in Christ Jesus. All Scripture is given by inspiration of God, and is profitable for doctrine, for reproof, for correction, for instruction in righteousness, that the man of God may be complete, thoroughly equipped for every good work* (2 Timothy 3:14-17).

Coming clean is life and death to those who want a God-given voice—a voice that drives back evil. Admit it! Modern American Christians are distracted and, in many cases, deceived. God is neither in their marketing programs nor in their diluted gospel of convenience. God is not in the circus atmosphere of false miracles and man-made prophecies.

If you regard the carnal church, God will not hear you. If you dabble in the gifts the way the New Age movement dabbles in crystals, God is deaf to your prayers. If you toy with the Holy Spirit in the same way that some use Tarot cards, then your prayers are an abomination.

What makes it so horrendous is that Christians are doing all of these things in the middle of a war. They are looking the other way as satan builds a prison for their children and grandchildren.

But there is a great hope. Power to destroy the works of satan is available. Training from the Holy Spirit to use the weapons of God awaits you. Heaven has a strategy, kept ready and waiting for our obedience. God wants to give you the greatest voice of all—prevailing prayer.

*But before there can be a great awakening, there must be a rude awakening.*

The people of Judah complained that all of their efforts to get God's attention had failed. God spoke through Isaiah and exposed their condition. They assumed that if they fasted, God would have to listen to them. They were about to get an education.

> *"Why have we fasted," they say, "and You have not seen? Why have we afflicted our souls, and You take no notice?"* (Isaiah 58:3)

God was not listening because they were trying to manipulate fasting. The prophet continues:

> *In fact, in the day of your fast you find pleasure, and exploit all your laborers. Indeed, you fast for strife and debate, and to strike with the fist of wickedness. You*

*will not fast as you do this day, to make your voice*
*heard on high. Is it a fast that I have chosen, a day for*
*a man to afflict his soul? Is it to bow down his head*
*like a bulrush, and to spread out sackcloth and ashes?*
*Would you call this a fast, and an acceptable day to*
*the Lord?* (Isaiah 58:3-5)

These are loaded questions! God asks, "Do you think that your 'Kabuki theater' prayers get results? Do you think I will reward you for putting on an act of self-denial?" Then God answers!

*Is this not the fast that I have chosen: to loose the bonds*
*of wickedness, to undo the heavy burdens, to let the*
*oppressed go free, and that you break every yoke? Is it*
*not to share your bread with the hungry, and that you*
*bring to your house the poor who are cast out; when*
*you see the naked, that you cover him, and not hide*
*yourself from your own flesh?* (Isaiah 58:6-7)

You can feel God's heart in this. "I can't hear you! You think prayer and fasting are a booster rocket for your pet projects. I am not in the empire you are trying to build. I have plans of My own!"

*Instead of going without food, God wanted them to give out food.* We have a destiny with the poor. Yes, the Left has done horrendous social work. Yes, they have left the poor worse off. But that does not mean we cannot touch the hungry and the homeless.

In fact, the Left rushed in to fill the vacuum left behind by the Church's failure. But the Left tried to fill the vacuum with cold institutional programs. We have had the edge all the time. We have compassion, and we can bring them love and dignity.

Nothing tells us more about the abject failure and insult of Leftist programs than this: At the beginning of Black History Month 2022 we learned that Joe Biden's Health and Human Services will be giving out "safe smoking kits" designed, in part, to help tobacco smokers, vapers, and crack addicts to smoke more safely. However, they have denied that taxpayer money will pay for crack pipes or that they are targeting minorities.

In our crusades, we do not just hand out sandwiches. Our workers pray with people. They see miracles of healing. Not only that, but we come back again and again. The poor and homeless know that this is not a photo op for us. We are genuinely committed to getting them off of the streets.

But this has another great benefit. Those who volunteer at our crusades are never the same. They go home to become the best gift a pastor ever had.

The final sin of those who were fasting was that their own families were not in order. "And do not hide yourself from your own flesh." How many famous Christian leaders have we seen who ignore their own marriage and their children? They show the love of God to everyone except the very ones God has given them to love.

Whenever the Church finds a shortcut for growth, the first two things that are cut out are prayer and soul-winning. Even when prayer is retained, it is kept as an artificial version of itself. We intercede with no intention of hearing and obeying God's orders. Where we fail is by thinking that intercession replaces obedience and by not matching our prayers with expectation of receiving marching orders. How can we obey what Jesus said in Matthew 9:38, "Therefore pray the Lord of the harvest to send out laborers into His harvest" and yet not expect to send workers into the harvest?

Such simple corrections! But such vast rewards! So much so that we are without excuse.

Here is what God promised to those who repent of false prayer and fasting:

> *Then your light shall break forth like the morning, your healing shall spring forth speedily, and your righteousness shall go before you; the glory of the Lord shall be your rear guard. Then you shall call, and the Lord will answer; you shall cry, and He will say, "Here am I"* (Isaiah 58:8-9).

But what was the final reward of those who will repent? Instead of the disappointment of silence, and after a lifetime of praying without seeing results, we will hear God say, "Here am I!"

## Notes

1. E.M. Bounds, *Power Through Prayer* (1910), Chapter 1.
2. Matthew Henry, *Matthew Henry Commentary on the Whole Bible,* "Marks of Perilous Times; Excellence of the Scriptures," II, https://www.biblestudytools.com/commentaries/matthew -henry-complete/2-timothy/3.html.

# Chapter 21

# FINDING YOUR GOD-GIVEN VOICE

*Of all the talents bestowed upon men, none is so precious as the gift of oratory. He who enjoys it wields a power more durable than that of a great king. He is an independent force in the world. Abandoned by his party, betrayed by his friends, stripped of his offices, whoever can command this power is still formidable.*
—Winston Churchill

AMERICA IS BEING FLOODED BY EVIL AND DEPRAVITY because the loudest voices are evil and depraved. They have the national microphones. They have silenced everyone else.

The Bible tells us the danger of the last days is not what nature will do but what men will be.

> *But know this, that in the last days perilous times will
> come: For men will be lovers of themselves, lovers of
> money, boasters, proud, blasphemers, disobedient to
> parents, unthankful, unholy, unloving, unforgiving,
> slanderers, without self-control, brutal, despisers of
> good, traitors, headstrong, haughty, lovers of pleasure
> rather than lovers of God* (2 Timothy 3:1-4).

America is being destroyed by voices. The power of voices to
do evil is terrifying. Hitler's oratory was just as destructive as any
of his other weapons.

If voices can destroy America, it follows then that God-given
voices can save her. We need voices, big and small, famous voices
and regular folks. We need them in the high places and in the
everyday places. They need to be in schools, businesses, government, entertainment centers. In short, everywhere.

You can be that voice. I will go even further. God has already
bestowed this gift on you—but you have to *find* it. Here is how
you begin.

*Start by recognizing God's choice. The God-given voice is
the weapon He has chosen for our national redemption.* Luke 21
proves this. Jesus is speaking to the disciples—talking to us every
bit as much as He was to them—about how to live in the last
days. He sobers them with the atrocities of the end times and
the hatred toward our faith. *Then God will open the door for
you to speak.*

> *But before all these things, they will lay their hands on
> you and persecute you, delivering you up to the syna-
> gogues and prisons. You will be brought before kings*

*and rulers for My name's sake. But it will turn out
for you as an occasion for testimony* (Luke 21:12-13).

No matter what, He says, it will turn. Amazing! No matter how intense the evil becomes, it will be forced to become an opportunity for God-empowered voices to speak.

This happened to Paul. They put him in prison, yet God forced it to be a witness.

*But I want you to know, brethren, that the things
which happened to me have actually turned out for the
furtherance of the gospel* (Philippians 1:12).

Right now, it may seem impossible to you. You cannot imagine yourself being a supernatural voice at a schoolboard meeting, or in an executive corporation meeting—or even to the media.

You may be terrified to speak in front of people. The devil may bring up your past. You may think that you are in a situation that makes it impossible to prepare to be used of God.

You may feel cast aside and trapped in horrible circumstances. You may feel that your true talents have been ignored. These are valid complaints, but they cannot stop God. He is able to blast you out of all of them! In fact, your circumstances are no big deal. The important change that is needed is not in your situation—it is in you.

*The Answer is the Holy Spirit. God's Spirit will come upon you
and you will be transformed.*

*Then the Spirit of the Lord will come upon you,
and you will prophesy with them and be turned into
another man. And let it be, when these signs come to*

*you, that you do as the occasion demands; for God is with you* (1 Samuel 10:6-7).

Your natural shyness will be overruled. Your fear of rejection will be removed. Your temperament will be transcended. Any confusion over what you should do will be replaced by a purposeful sense of direction. You will do as the occasion demands, for God is with you!

Now it becomes apparent that the God-given voice has always been the weapon of choice in impossible situations. The Church was never more vulnerable than after Christ died and rose again. Those early believers were huddled in an upper room, filled with uncertainty.

Before He ascended, Jesus had told them about the transformation which was coming.

*But you shall receive power when the Holy Spirit has come upon you; and you shall be witnesses to Me in Jerusalem, and in all Judea and Samaria, and to the end of the earth* (Acts 1:8).

Then He told them to wait.

So, they waited. Almost to mock them, Jerusalem was celebrating the Feast of Pentecost. The city was filled with visitors from all over the known world. The 120 believers could not have felt more disregarded. Yet within a few hours the tables would turn completely.

First, there was a mighty rushing wind. Then, tongues of fire sat on them. They were baptized in the Holy Spirit, and they overflowed into the streets. Their voices were something the world had never heard before. They were speaking in languages supernaturally. They were using words and patterns of words that people heard, and they were shocked to hear that these Jews knew each of their languages. In the blink of an eye, the fledgling Church became a global dynamo. And you can become one too!

*But the gift is far more than words. It is wisdom and irresistible arguments.*

Jesus said in Luke 21:14-15:

> *Therefore settle it in your hearts not to meditate beforehand on what you will answer; for I will give you a mouth and wisdom which all your adversaries will not be able to contradict or resist.*

You will find yourself able to absorb information about which schoolboard meeting to attend, which politician to contact, what group to join or volunteer for in order to use your voice. Then you will find yourself confident and supernaturally prepared because the Holy Spirit will be the One who is empowering and guiding you!

You will find yourself fearless and commanding. You will confront evildoers and those who would try to censor you. The power of God will even silence mobs and neutralize them with the truth. It is what Paul said in 2 Corinthians 10:5:

> *Casting down arguments and every high thing that exalts itself against the knowledge of God, bringing every thought into captivity to the obedience of Christ.*

*How do you find your God-given voice?* Your message to America is even now smoldering in your moral outrage. What is angering you? What is breaking your heart? Where do you feel the pain? The word of the Lord is maturing inside you like a flame.

> *Then I said, "I will not make mention of Him, nor speak anymore in His name." But His word was in my heart like a burning fire shut up in my bones; I was weary of holding it back, but I could not* (Jeremiah 20:9).

You find your God-given voice in fervent prayer. It is the warrior's cry. It is the force of a child of God who has seen enough and must act. It is the crushing realization of a threat that must be met head-on with something outside ourselves.

Peter said it best in Acts 4:29: "Now, Lord, look on their threats, and grant to Your servants that with all boldness they may speak Your word."

And it is what Peter asked for next that we will study in the next chapter—something that is even greater than words.

Chapter 22

# PROVING YOUR MESSAGE IS FROM GOD

*If Paul had preached and taught without signs and wonders
following, his message would not have had its full impact.*
—DAVID WILKERSON

AMERICA'S CRISIS IS NOW BEYOND WORDS. WORDS ARE NOT
enough for a nation poisoned by rage and division. All civil discourse has been eradicated. For this generation to hear us, our
words must be verified by miracles. Paul said:

> *And my speech and my preaching were not with
> persuasive words of human wisdom, but in demonstration of the Spirit and of power, that your faith
> should not be in the wisdom of men but in the power
> of God* (1 Corinthians 2:4-5).

Miracles will let this generation hear your God-given voice. Many books on theology have tried in vain to explain the role of the supernatural. But it is amazing how much light the Bible—when it is allowed to speak for itself—can shed on commentaries:

> *Therefore they stayed there a long time, speaking boldly in the Lord, who was bearing witness to the word of His grace, granting signs and wonders to be done by their hands* (Acts 14:3).

I also like this paraphrase:

> *Nevertheless, they stayed there a long time, preaching boldly, and the Lord proved their message was from him by giving them power to do great miracles* (Acts 14:3 TLB).

"The Lord proved their message was from him." Miracles prove your message is from God. Paul clearly did not believe we can fully preach the Gospel without miracles.

> *In mighty signs and wonders, by the power of the Spirit of God, so that from Jerusalem and round about to Illyricum I have fully preached the gospel of Christ* (Romans 15:19).

David Wilkerson said: "If Paul had preached and taught without signs and wonders following, his message would not have had its full impact. It would not have been the gospel fully preached!"[1]

A message from God crowned with miracles delivers a devastating blow to evil. That is why satan hates miracles and has driven the Church to extremes when it comes to the supernatural. One extreme denies that miracles are for today. The other extreme behaves with such fakery and emotionalism that they discredit the gifts of the Spirit.

> *Truly the signs of an apostle were accomplished among you with all perseverance, in signs and wonders and mighty deeds* (2 Corinthians 12:12).

This is a powerful verse, but today these words are offensive to many because of the abuses. Commenting on this, David Wilkerson said:

> Note Paul's words in this verse: signs, wonders, mighty deeds. Most Christians today cringe when they hear these words! Why? Because these words have been made an abomination by unscrupulous, power-hungry preachers and teachers! The great tragedy is that such perversions have caused many God-fearing pastors, evangelists and laypeople to turn away from the truth of a fully preached gospel.[2]

## THE GREAT TRAGEDY

David Wilkerson was saying something that was earthshaking. We aren't powerless because of charlatans and fakes. We are powerless because good people are reacting to those charlatans and fakes.

Should we be fighting the battle of our lives without our best weapons? *What?* Because some have misused them?

The Bible says, "For the weapons of our warfare are not carnal but mighty in God for pulling down strongholds" (2 Cor. 10:4).

We can't say that about our current weapons—because they are not weapons, they are marketing tools. And that makes us pathetic.

Sermons that might have forked lightning and turned a city to God merely flatten into harmless speeches. Events that might have destroyed demonic strongholds are, instead, concerts with motivational talks. Utterly useless against the evil that is killing America.

We are not fooling anybody with our empty gospel. Secular America intuitively knows something is wrong with us. They can smell compromise. They can see the contradiction between our claims and our condition.

Are you sick of this mess? Do you want power? Power that evicts devils and destroys the arguments of wicked men? Are you in pain because you see evil prevailing and you feel helpless to do anything about it? Then let's do something about it!

The best news is that you *can* do something about it! The God-given voice and the anointing to verify it with miracles is not just for preachers. It is for every believer!

> *And these signs will follow those who believe: In My name they will cast out demons; they will speak with new tongues; they will take up serpents; and if they drink anything deadly, it will by no means hurt them; they will lay hands on the sick, and they will recover* (Mark 16:17-18).

The nine gifts of the Spirit are for all of the Church. The quickening of wisdom to speak irresistible words is not just for pulpits. God wants that power flowing in every tongue and in every endeavor undertaken for the glory of Christ.

God wants all His soldiers to take supernatural power into every sphere—business, education, law enforcement, entertainment, and yes, into the ministry.

This is more urgent today than ever. We are watching the wholesale destruction of decency and freedom. We dare not be silent and we dare not go out in our own power. We must ask for gifts. We must yearn for gifts and make the proper application of them our lifelong study. The bottom line is that God wants you to have power, wisdom, and bold authority.

Our quest to have these power gifts work in us is mapped out in Acts 4:29-30:

> *Now, Lord, look on their threats, and grant to Your servants that with all boldness they may speak Your word, by stretching out Your hand to heal, and that signs and wonders may be done through the name of Your holy Servant Jesus.*

## Behold the Threat

You cannot talk to God about a threat you are ignorant of or that you do not believe is a threat. The threat is real. The authorities told Peter to silence his God-given voice.

They ordered him to stop doing miracles. Naturally, he prayed for more of what got him arrested—boldness to speak, as well as for more miracles.

This threat is too big and too immediate for us to put off. We must face it, now. We must bring it to God. Peter is clearly saying, "O Lord! Look and what they have done. Look at the slavery they are threatening us with. This will affect our children! We cannot ignore it!"

*Give us boldness to tell all of the truth!* We want the message that is from You, O Lord. We want to declare it without hesitation.

We do not want to color it, dilute it, or leave anything out that You want us to say.

Dear reader, can you pray that, and mean it?

*We do not want just any kind of boldness.* We want the special boldness that comes when miracles confirm our message. We want the signs and wonders that take us to boldness!

Previously, I quoted 1 Samuel 10:6-7:

> *Then the Spirit of the Lord will come upon you, and you will prophesy with them and be turned into another man. And let it be, when these signs come to you, that you do as the occasion demands; for God is with you.*

I told you before that it all begins with an outpouring of the Holy Spirit. That is exactly what happened in direct answer to Peter's prayer.

> *And when they had prayed, the place where they were assembled together was shaken; and they were all filled with the Holy Spirit, and they spoke the word of God with boldness (Acts 4:31).*

T.L Osborn said, "The Gospel of the Kingdom must be preached with evidence; it must be preached as a witness. This can only be done by Christians who are filled with the Holy Spirit."

The Holy Spirit is your power, confidence, wisdom, and helper. He is the One who will transform you. He is the One who will not only give you the words, He will show you how to study. Yes, you need to study! Remember what Paul said to Timothy:

*Be diligent to present yourself approved to God, a worker who does not need to be ashamed, rightly dividing the word of truth* (2 Timothy 2:15).

You will not necessarily deliver a prepared speech. But the Spirit of God will quicken your voice by drawing words and phrases from your studies, and He will arm you with arguments that tear down lies.

*Casting down arguments and every high thing that exalts itself against the knowledge of God, bringing every thought into captivity to the obedience of Christ* (2 Corinthians 10:5).

He will also show you when and where to give your message. You will feel power while you are speaking. The Holy Spirit will impart right answers, and they will be lightning fast and irresistible.

*Therefore settle it in your hearts not to meditate beforehand on what you will answer; for I will give you a mouth and wisdom which all your adversaries will not be able to contradict or resist* (Luke 21:14-15).

The Spirit of God will be your strategist. He will be your confidence. He will reveal who you can trust and who to avoid.

How do I know that you will see signs and wonders? How do I know that your fervent prayer will be answered? The answer is that your yearning for these things to come is the guarantee of their coming. Matthew 5:6 shows us this truth, "Blessed are those who hunger and thirst for righteousness, for they shall be filled." You are blessed if you hunger because the hunger is the proof of the fulfillment.

Why would you let America die? Why would anyone leave quietly who is enraged by the evil, who has fire in them to do something about it, who knows that the Holy Spirit can come upon them and fill them with an irresistible tongue and a battery of mighty weapons—with the promise of victory from the highest source? God is going to prove that your message is from Him. That proof will pierce the darkness.

## Notes

1. David Wilkerson, "The Fully Preached Gospel," sermon, https://www.sermonindex.net/modules/articles/index .php?view=article&aid=27673.
2. Ibid.

# Chapter 23

# HOW OUR WEAPONS BECOME MIGHTY

YOU HAVE DECLARED YOURSELF. YOU HAVE TOLD HEAVEN and earth that you will not leave quietly. But how do you do damage to evil? How do you keep from being one more casualty on the battlefield? The real soldier asks those questions with transparent honesty.

Jesus showed us how. He said in John 5:19, "Most assuredly, I say to you, the Son can do nothing of Himself, but what He sees the Father do; for whatever He does, the Son also does in like manner."

Wicked plans disintegrated when they came into contact with Christ, because His every move was limited to what He saw His Father doing.

The lethal warrior does nothing that is unproven in combat. Plans, weapons, and opportunities are not enough. Warriors shun everything except those things that actually work against the enemy. There are only certain things they can do. They are careful to only do those things.

Our weapons become mighty when we strictly adhere to the Bible and the Holy Spirit.

I want to make some very serious points about you and your warfare.

*You must understand modern evil before you can defeat it.*

> *Finally, my brethren, be strong in the Lord and in the power of His might. Put on the whole armor of God, that you may be able to stand against the wiles of the devil. For we do not wrestle against flesh and blood, but against principalities, against powers, against the rulers of the darkness of this age, against spiritual hosts of wickedness in the heavenly places. Therefore take up the whole armor of God, that you may be able to withstand in the evil day, and having done all, to stand* (Ephesians 6:10-13).

We must look evil square in the eye. We must grasp the totality of evil. Only after we understand how it thinks and breathes can we qualify to defeat it. And Leftist evil is in a class all its own.

The evil we face today and how to defeat it is showcased in Acts 3 and 4. It opens with an undeniable miracle of healing. In fact, the narrative goes out of its way to confirm how undeniable this healing is.

*First there is the reaction of the people of Jerusalem.*

> *And all the people saw him walking and praising God. Then they knew that it was he who sat begging alms at the Beautiful Gate of the temple; and they were filled with wonder and amazement at what had happened to him* (Acts 3:9-10).

*This is further confirmed even by those who hated the miracle.* Caiaphas and the other priests and leaders said in Acts 4:16:

> *What are we to do with these men? For the fact that an extraordinary miracle has taken place through them is public knowledge and clearly evident to all the residents of Jerusalem, and we cannot deny it* (AMP).

"We cannot deny it." But what does evil do in the face of the undeniable power of God? The answer is mind-bending.

They had just admitted the healing was irrefutable. But in their next breath they say, "But." How can there be a "but" about anything that makes cripples walk? The Jewish leaders went on to say:

> *But so that it spreads no further among the people, let us severely threaten them, that from now on they speak to no man in this name* (Acts 4:17).

Evil people will try to stay in power no matter what. Facts, science, proof, and even God goes out the window if it means they will lose power. Note the phrase, "an extraordinary miracle has taken place *through* them." They are not just admitting that a genuine healing has taken place, but that God did it *through* Peter. *But,* in order to stay in power, they even have to oppose God.

Shocking, right? Well, they did this before, and that time it was a much greater miracle.

Remember their reaction to Lazarus being raised from the dead? Everyone else was rejoicing that a corpse, which had been dead four days, was raised by Jesus. At that time, Caiaphas said,

"If we let Him alone like this, everyone will believe in Him, and the Romans will come and take away both our place and nation" (John 11:48).

*Notice their order of priority*—they said, "our place," even before they said anything about "the nation." *Sound familiar?* Can you think of any American leaders who would rather let America die before they would surrender their power? And surely no politician who had witnessed the power of God would dream of banning it. Right?

Government programs have a paltry cure rate of around 7 percent for drug addicts. Their defeatism is so glaring that they are now just giving away needles and "safety kits." By contrast, programs that include the baptism of the Holy Spirit have a cure rate around 80 percent. *But* (there's that word again), because these programs are Christian, the government will not utilize them in the war on drugs. Demonstrating that they are no different from Caiaphas.

Moreover, the Sanhedrin treated the Christian faith as if it were a virus: "*But* so that it *spreads no further.*"

Our leaders are doing that today, but not openly. At least the priests in the Book of Acts were honest about it.

The Leftist politicians in power want you to believe they are trying to stop the coronavirus. However, Jane Fonda called the virus, "God's gift to the Left." In that, she's right. To them it is not even a virus. It is a gift. An excuse for the greatest power grab in American history. And it is even more insidious than that.

*The Left considers faith and freedom to be infections.*

COVID-19 was never the target. To them, faith and freedom are the infections. The evidence is clear. Why else would they keep doing lockdowns, masks, and injections, knowing they don't work?

If coronavirus was the threat they claim it to be, they would not be pouring hundreds of thousands of illegals into our cities without any COVID-19 tests, shots, or masks. These leaders don't wear masks when no one is looking. They know they do not work. They really do believe we are stupid.

Now look at this. Jesus sent the disciples out with this mandate, "And as you go, preach, saying, 'The kingdom of heaven is at hand.' Heal the sick, cleanse the lepers, raise the dead, cast out demons. Freely you have received, freely give" (Matthew 10:7-8).

Okay, how would anyone reject the Gospel after seeing various incurable diseases such as leprosy being healed and after seeing the dead raised? Yet in verse 14, Jesus said, "And whoever will not receive you nor hear your words, when you depart from that house or city, shake off the dust from your feet."

*Wait, what?* No wonder Jesus called it a greater evil than Sodom and Gomorrah.

To stand in the evil day means you will never stop. You will never back down. And you will not allow their rejection of the truth to stop you from speaking up.

You must act *essential.* Tear off the labels that the Left puts on you.

> *And when they had set them in the midst, they asked,*
> *"By what power or by what name have you done this?"*
> *Then Peter, filled with the Holy Spirit, said to them,*
> *"Rulers of the people and elders of Israel: If we this day*

*are judged for a good deed done to a helpless man, by what means he has been made well, let it be known to you all, and to all the people of Israel, that by the name of Jesus Christ of Nazareth, whom you cruci-fied, whom God raised from the dead, by Him this man stands here before you whole"* (Acts 4:7-10).

They judged the miracle to be a crime. Peter called it a good deed. False politeness and acting intimidated is how the American Church left quietly. But in the first century, Peter would have none of it!

Act *essential!* We belong in the halls of power and in main-stream America. We are not a conspiracy theory or a fringe group. And there are too many of us to be labeled just a "remnant."

We should not be embarrassed.

We must remember that Christ is the undisputed champion of every social ill. No one is serious about human rights if they leave Him out. Nobody is sincere in dealing with addiction, hatred, or racism if they ignore His power and the testimony of Christianity.

*Before anyone else, we of the household of God need to be con-vinced of this.* Because the disciples were convinced, they were also convincing.

*Now when they saw the boldness of Peter and John, and perceived that they were uneducated and untrained men, they marveled. And they realized that they had been with Jesus* (Acts 4:13).

You belong in media. You belong in politics. You belong in corporate board meetings. We all belong in the power centers of America. Our voice should be heard loudly, clearly, and continually.

And finally, *we must take our case directly to the people.* We have seen that evil leaders may never yield, no matter how much proof we provide them. That is why we must go directly to the people. This must become a populist movement. "Everyday people" are an amazing force. The following verses demonstrate the firewall that regular folk can be.

> *So when they had further threatened them, they let them go, finding no way of punishing them, because of the people, since they all glorified God for what had been done* (Acts 4:21).
>
> *So one came and told them, saying, "Look, the men whom you put in prison are standing in the temple and teaching the people!" Then the captain went with the officers and brought them without violence, for they feared the people, lest they should be stoned* (Acts 5:25-26).

Irresistible words of wisdom and confrontation automatically appear in the mouth of the Spirit-filled warrior when he is summoned before men.

> *Then Peter, filled with the Holy Spirit, said to them, "Rulers of the people and elders of Israel"* (Acts 4:8).

Gifts of healing and working of miracles naturally overtake the bold preaching of the Gospel.

Why would we choose to be powerless when God is inviting us to be mighty? Why would we continue to use methods and ideas that have failed horribly? The way has been opened for us to properly use the weapons of God to the tearing down of strongholds. Let us seize His way.

Let us settle for nothing less.

# ABOUT MARIO MURILLO

MARIO MURILLO ROSE FROM POVERTY IN THE MISSION District of San Francisco. After being revolutionized by Christ, he felt a call to the riot-torn University of California at Berkeley. He was rejected until a desperate prayer season resulted in supernatural power. It began with preaching that was far different from any those students had ever heard before. Then the students began to report healings accomplished in the name of Jesus. A four-day crusade in San Jose, California that lasted six months with a total of over 250,000 people birthed an international ministry that is reaching millions!

# YOUR Prophetic COMMUNITY

## Are you passionate about hearing God's voice, walking with Jesus, and experiencing the power of the Holy Spirit?

Destiny Image is a community of believers with a passion for equipping and encouraging you to live the prophetic, supernatural life you were created for!

We offer a fresh helping of practical articles, dynamic podcasts, and powerful videos from respected, Spirit-empowered, Christian leaders to fuel the holy fire within you.